A-Z Street Atlas of MEDWAY TOWN

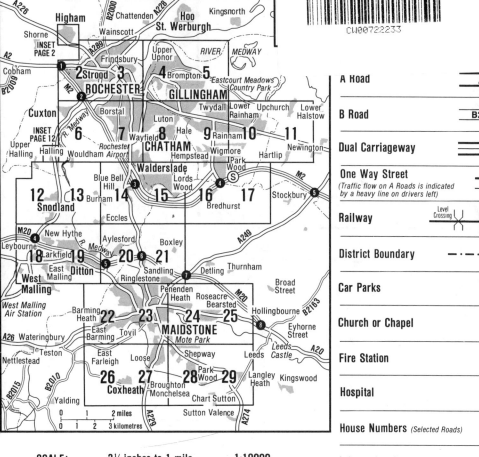

A Road	A2
B Road	B2004
Dual Carriageway	
One Way Street (Traffic flow on A Roads is indicated by a heavy line on drivers left)	
Railway	Level Crossing Station
District Boundary	
Car Parks	P
Church or Chapel	†
Fire Station	■
Hospital	Ⓗ
House Numbers (Selected Roads)	2 23
Information Centre	ℹ
National Grid Reference	¹60
Police Station	▲
Post Office	★
Toilet	▽
(Disabled Toilet-National Key Scheme)	♿

SCALE: 3⅓ inches to 1 mile   1:19000

0   ¼   ½   ¾ mile
0   250   500   750 metres   1 kilometre

© Copyright by the Publishers

Geographers' A-Z Map Company Limited

Head Office: Vestry Road, Sevenoaks, Kent, TN14 5EP.   Telephone 0732 451152
Showrooms: 44 Gray's Inn Road, Holborn, London, WC1X 8LR.   Telephone 01 242 9246

This Map is based upon the Ordnance Survey 1:10,000 & 1:10,560 Maps
with the sanction of the Controller of Her Majesty's Stationery Office.
Crown Copyright Reserved.

EDITION 1 1988
EDITION 1A (Part Revision) 1988

ISBN 0 85039 225 X

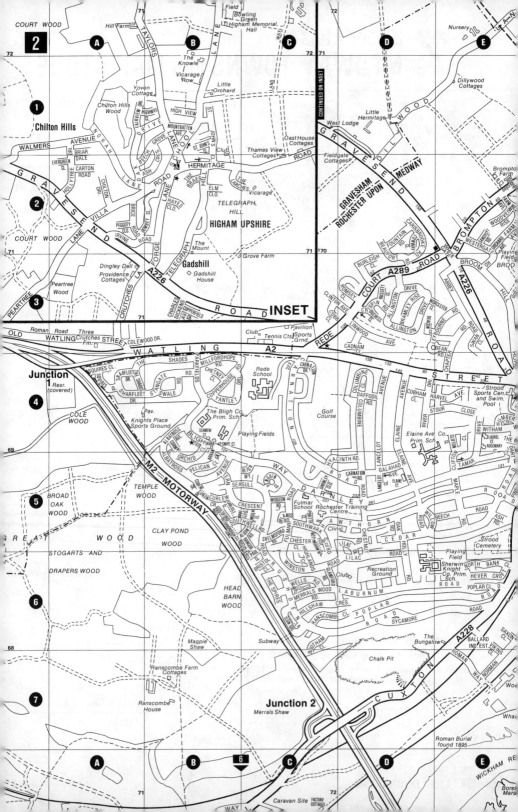

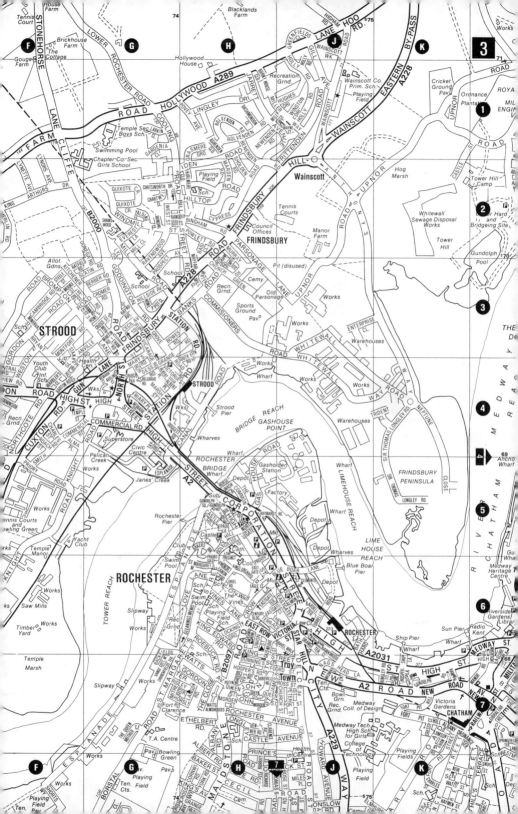

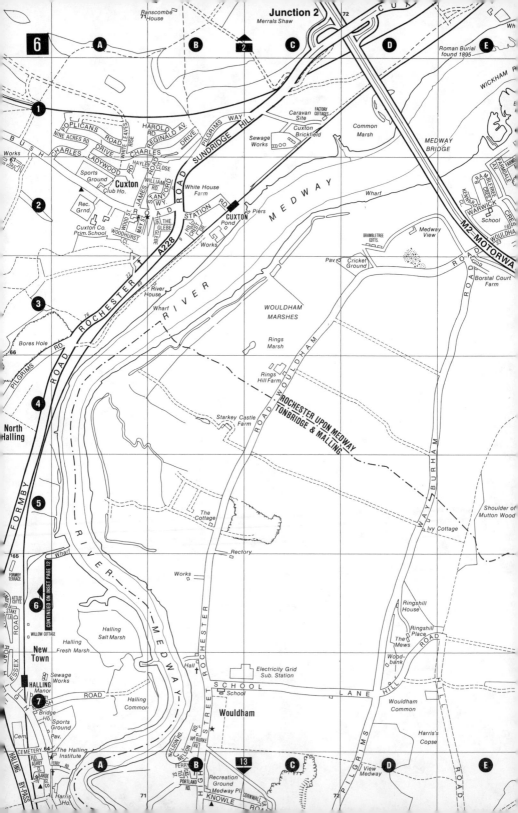

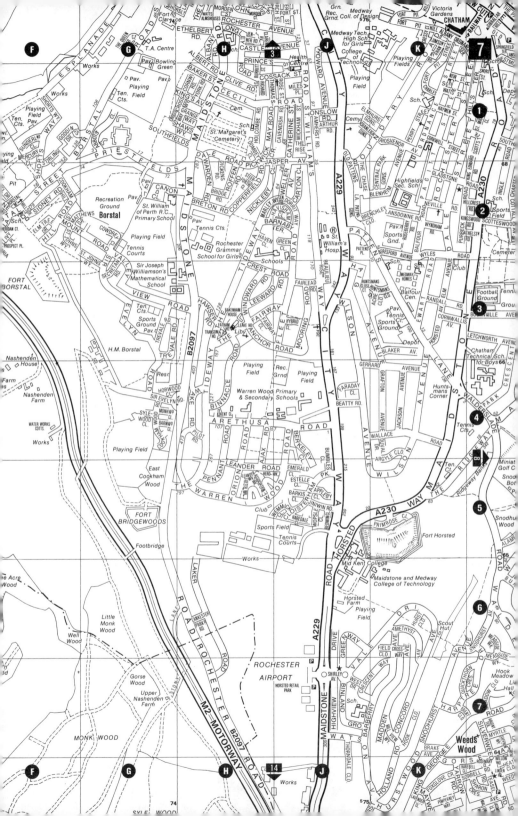

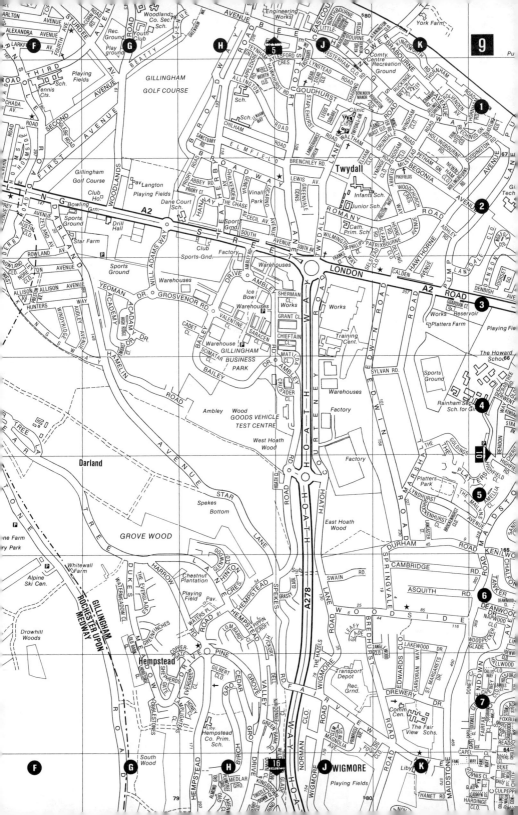

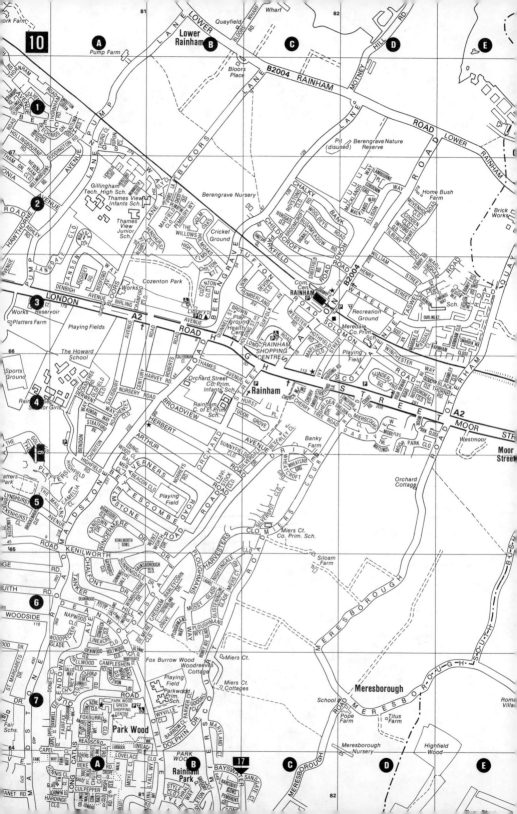

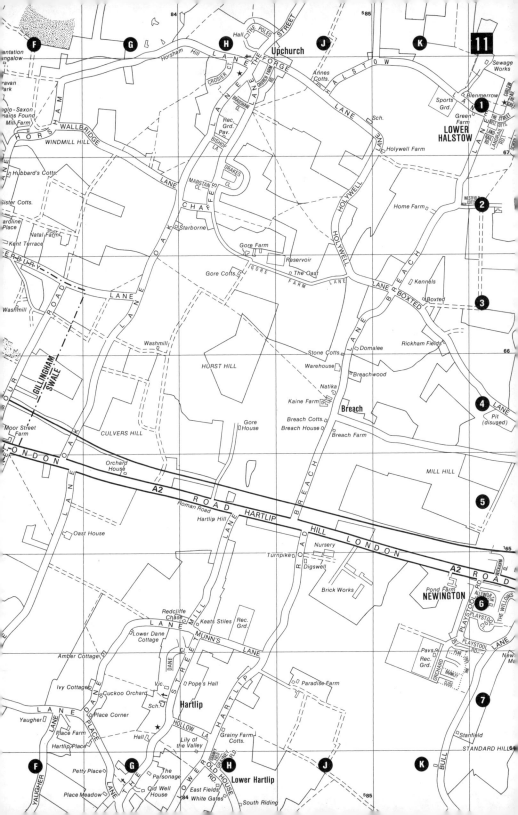

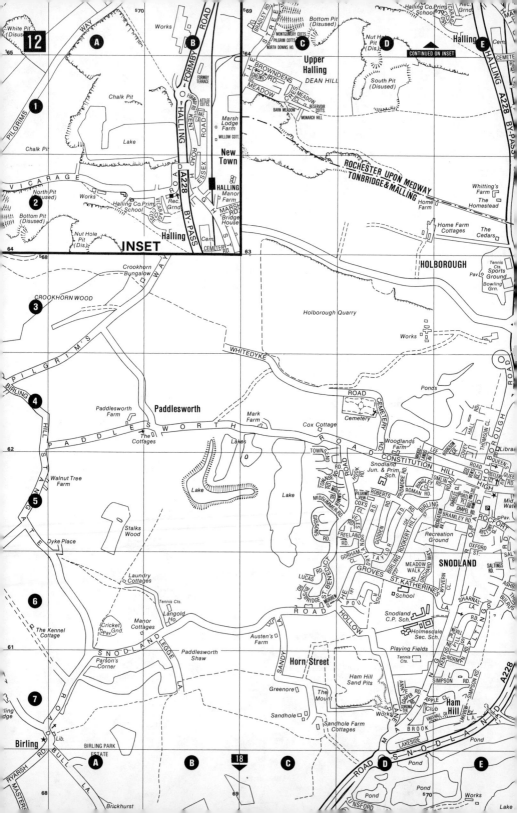

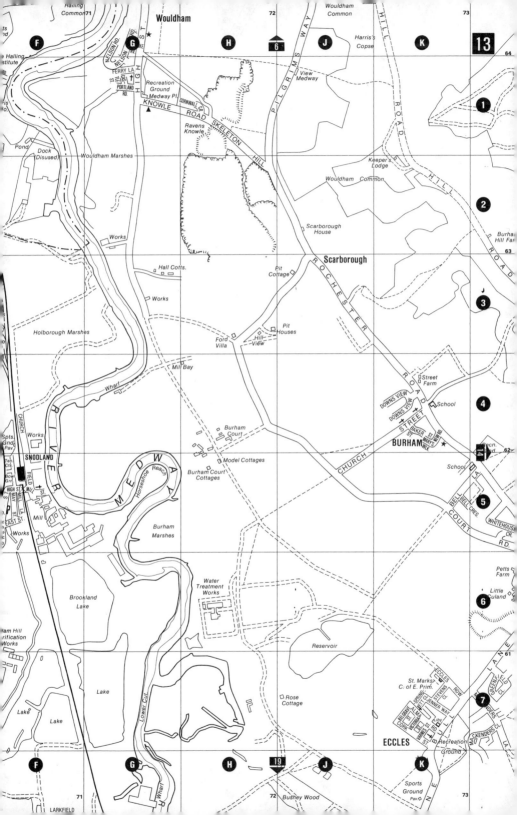

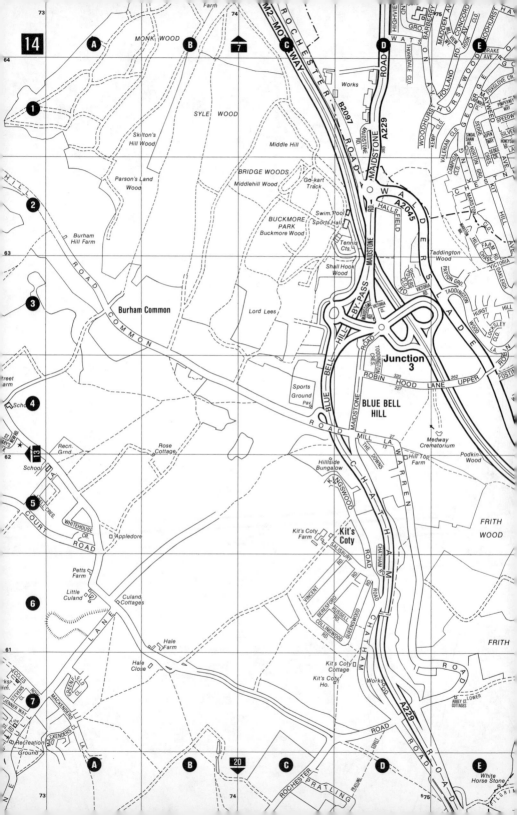

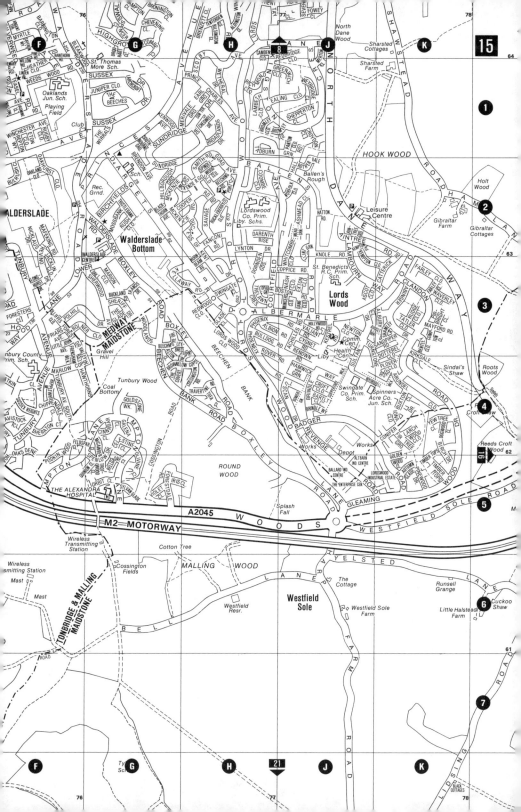

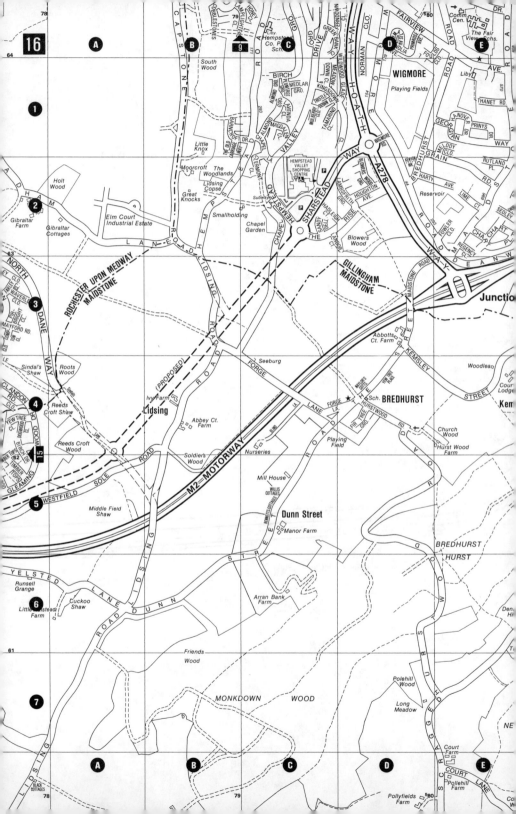

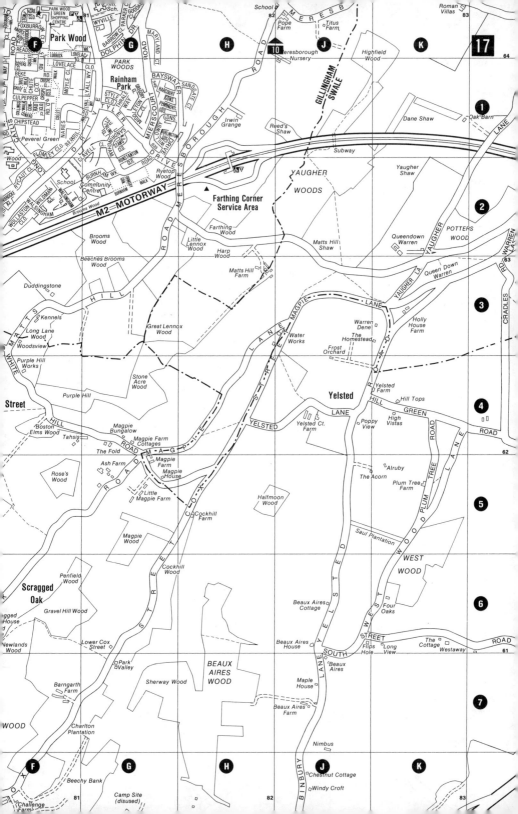

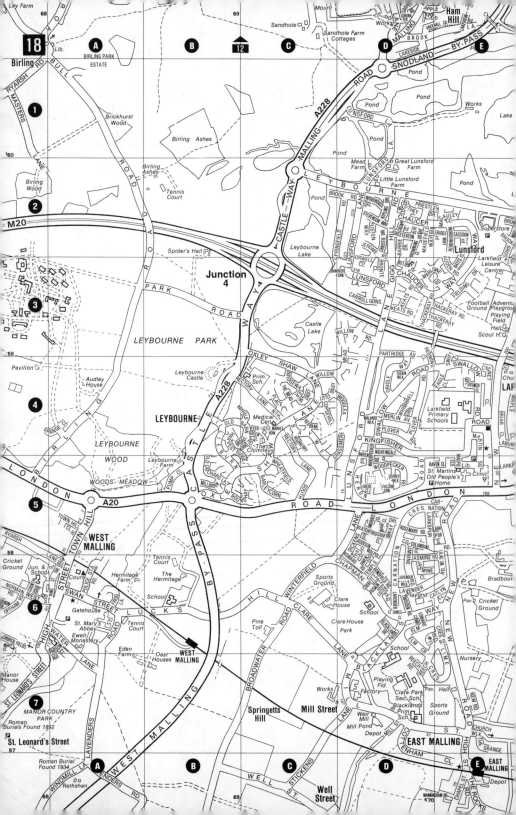

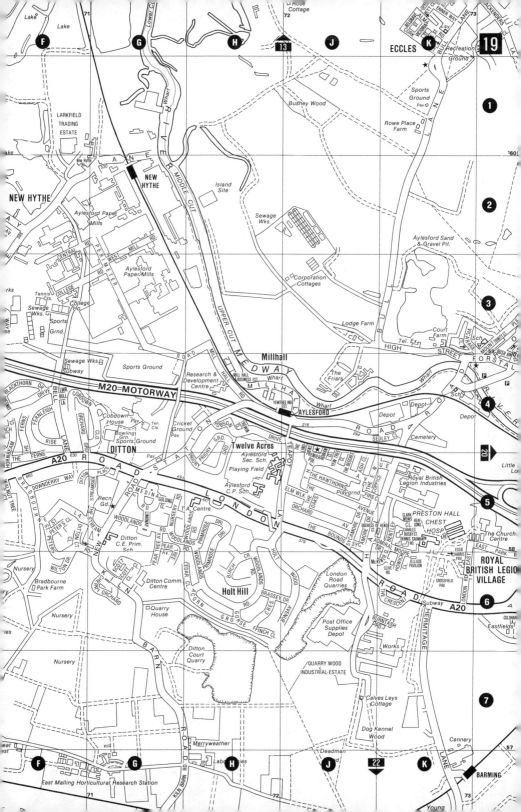

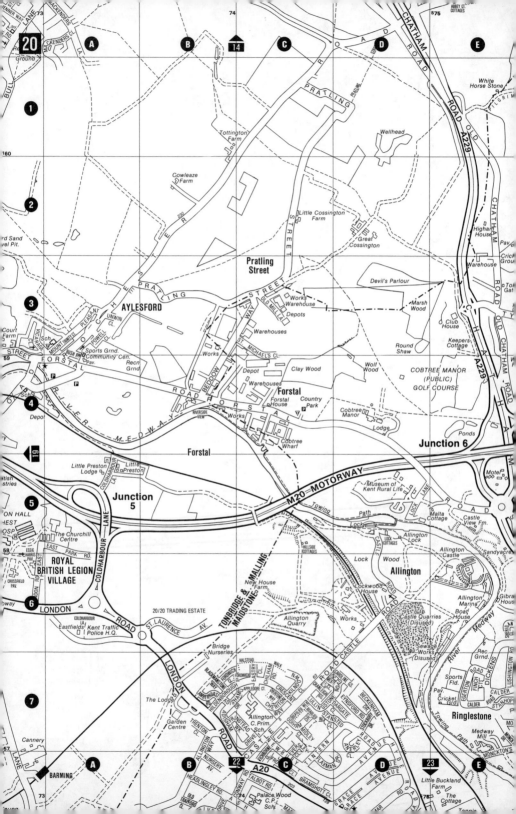

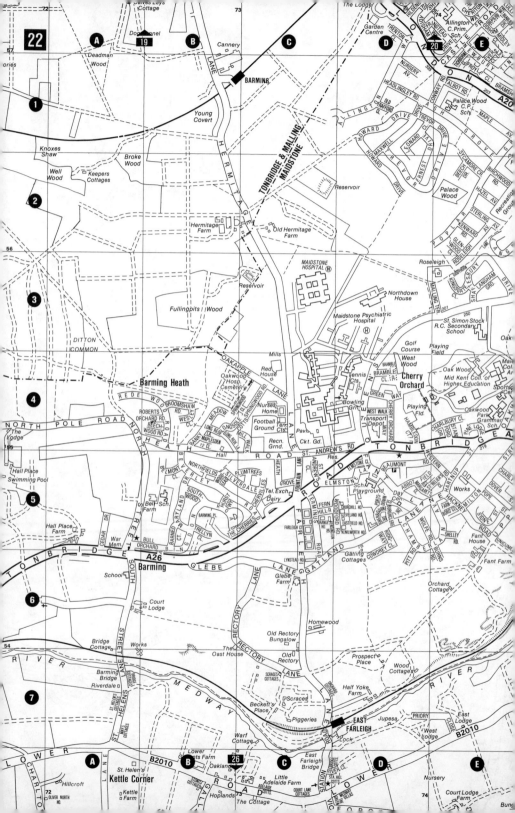

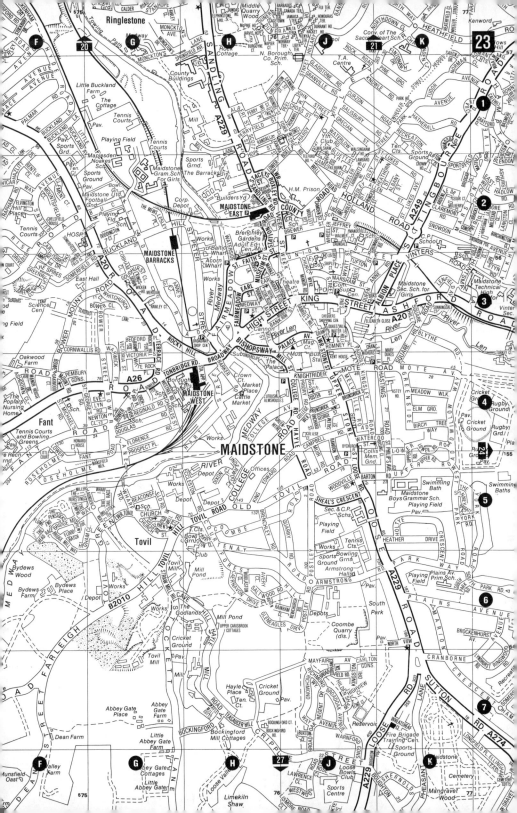

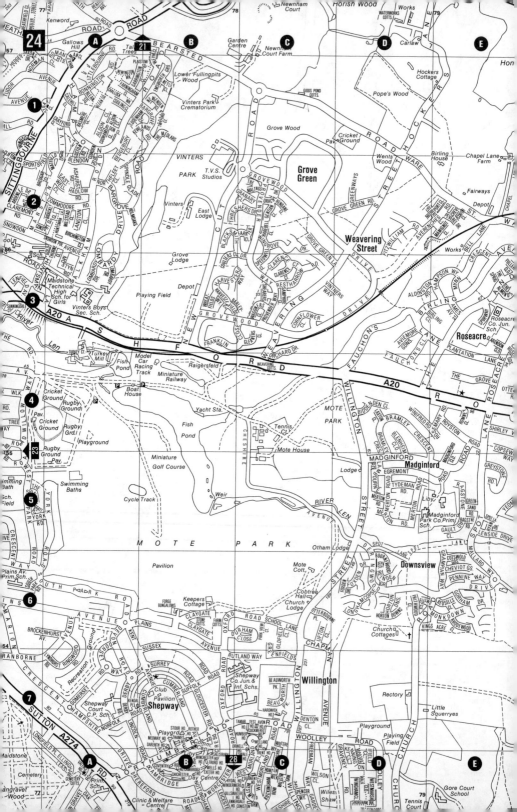

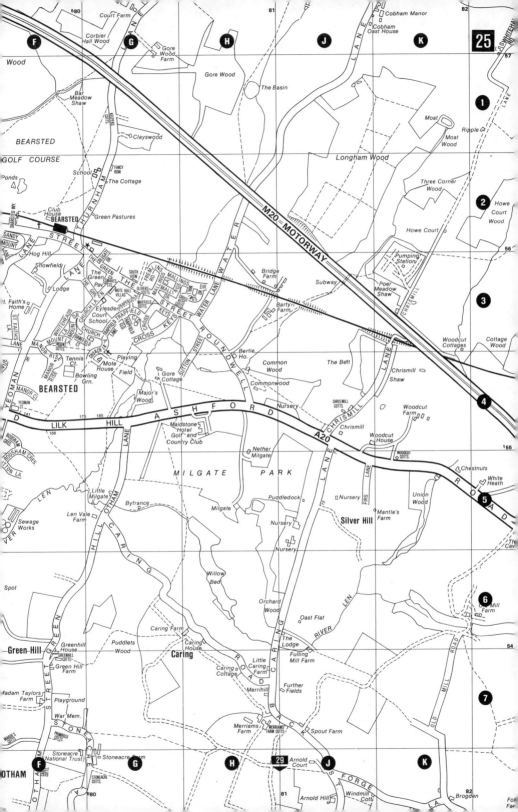

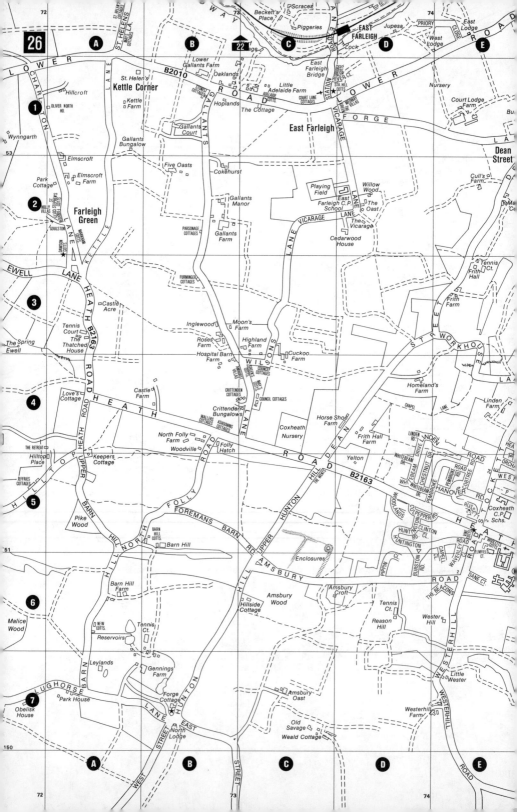

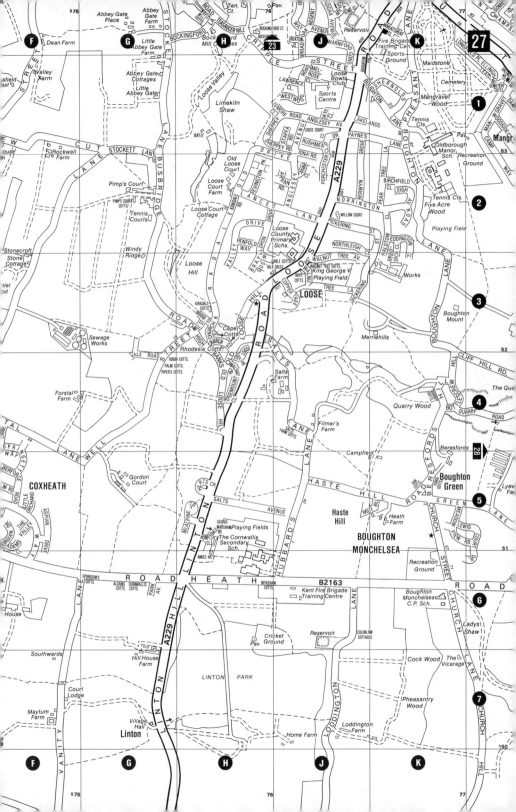

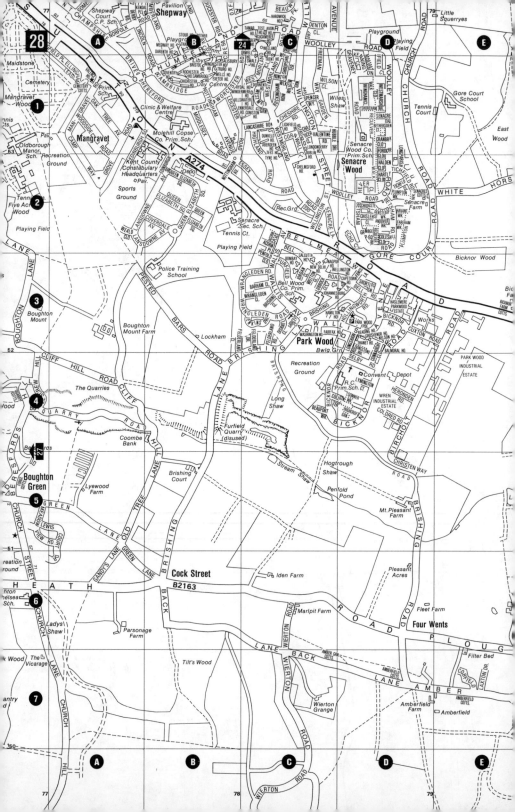

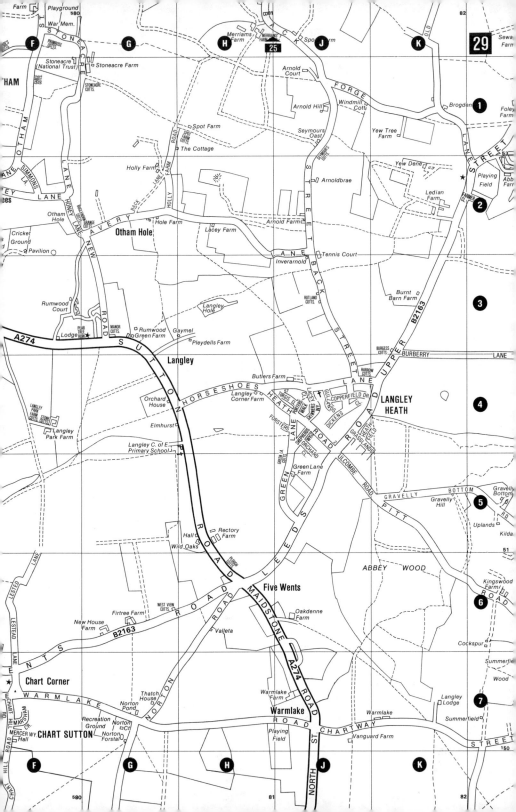

INDEX TO STREETS

HOW TO USE THIS INDEX

1. Each street name is followed by its Postal District and then by its map page reference; e.g. Abbey Ct. ME14—5F 21 is in the Medway 14 Postal District and it is to be found in square 5F on page 21. However, with the now general usage of Postal Coding, it is not recommended that this index should be used as a means of addressing mail.

2. A strict alphabetical order is followed in which Av., Rd., St. etc. (even though abbreviated) are read in full and as part of the street name, e.g. Amber Grn. Cotts. appears after Amberfield Cotts. but before Amber La.

3. Streets & Subsidiary names not shown on the Maps, appear in the Index in Italics with the thoroughfare to which it is connected shown in brackets.

GENERAL ABBREVIATIONS

All : Alley
App : Approach
Arc : Arcade
Av : Avenue
Bk : Back
Boulevd : Boulevard
Bri : Bridge
B'way : Broadway
Bldgs : Buildings
Chu : Church
Chyd : Churchyard
Circ : Circle
Cir : Circus
Clo : Close

Comn : Common
Cotts : Cottages
Ct : Court
Cres : Crescent
Dri : Drive
E : East
Embkmt : Embankment
Est : Estate
Gdns : Gardens
Ga : Gate
Gt : Great
Grn : Green
Gro : Grove
Ho : House

Ind : Industrial
Junct : Junction
La : Lane
Lit : Little
Lwr : Lower
Mnr : Manor
Mans : Mansions
Mkt : Market
ME : Medway
M : Mews
Mt : Mount
N : North
Pal : Palace
Pde : Parade

Pk : Park
Pas : Passage
Pl : Place
Rd : Road
S : South
Sq : Square
Sta : Station
St : Street
Ter : Terrace
TN : Tonbridge
Up : Upper
Vs : Villas
Wlk : Walk
W : West
Yd : Yard

Abbeville Ho. ME1—7H 3
Abbey Ct. ME14—5F 21
Abbey Ct. Cotts. ME20—7E 14
Abbey Ga. Cotts. ME14—4F 21
Abbey Rd. ME2—3E 2
Abbey Rd. ME8—2H 9
Abbot Field. ME16—5D 22
Abbots Clo. ME1—1G 7
Aberdeen Ho. ME15—1C 28
Abinger Dri. ME5—3K 15
Academy Dri. ME7—3G 9
Achilles Rd. ME5—3J 15
Acorn Gro. ME20—6H 19
Acorn Pl. ME15—2C 28
Acorn Rd. ME7—7G 5
Acre Clo. ME4—3K 7
Adams Clo. ME1—5F 27
Addison Clo. ME19—5D 18
Adelaide Cotts. ME15—1C 26
Adelaide Rd. ME7—7D 4
Adisham Dri. ME16—7B 20
Admiral Moore Dri. ME20—5K 19
Admiralty Rd. ME2—2A 4
Admiralty Ter. ME2—2A 4
Admiralty Ter. ME4—4B 4
Afghan Rd. ME4—7K 3
Aintree Rd. ME5—2J 15
Ajax Rd. ME1—4H 7
Alamein Av. ME5—5H 8
Albany Rd. ME1—7H 3
Albany Rd. ME4—2C 8
Albany Rd. ME7—7E 4
Albany St. ME14—2K 23
Albany Ter. ME4—7K 3
Albany Ter. ME7—7E 4
Albatross Av. ME2—4B 2
Albermarle Rd. ME5—3H 15
Albert Mnr. ME7—6C 4
Albert Pl. ME2—4G 3
Albert Rd. ME1—7H 3
Albert Rd. ME4—1B 8
Albert Rd. ME7—7D 4
Albert St. ME14—1H 23
Albion Pl. ME2—1B 4
Albion Pl. ME4—3K 23
Albion Rd. ME5—3H 15
Albury Clo. ME5—3K 15
Alchins Cotts. ME17—6G 27
Aldershot Rd. ME5—5B 8
Aldington Clo. ME5—7C 8
Aldington Rd. ME14—3D 24
Aldon Clo. ME14—1A 24
Aldon Ct. ME14—1A 24
Alexandra Av. ME7—7F 5
Alexandra Rd. ME4—2C 8
Alexandra St. ME14—1H 23
Alfred Clo. ME4—2C 8
Alkham Rd. ME14—3A 24
Allen Clo. ME5—6D 8
Allen St. ME14—2K 23
Allington Dri. ME2—3D 2
Allington Rd. ME8—1H 9
Allington Way. ME16—1D 22
Allison Av. ME7—2F 9
Allsworth Clo. ME9—6K 11
Alma Pl. ME2—4F 3
Alma Rd. ME20—7K 13

Almond Gro. ME7—1C 16
Almonds, The. ME14—3E 24
Almon Pl. ME1—6J 3
Altarn Ind. Centre. ME5—5J 15
Amanda Clo. ME5—2F 15
Amberfield Cotts. ME17
                —7D & 7E 28
Amber Grn. Cotts. ME17—7C 28
Amber La. ME17—7D 28
Amber Way. ME17—7F 29
  (off Amber La.)
Ambley Rd. ME7 & ME8—3H 9
Ames Av. ME14—3E 24
Amethyst Av. ME5—6K 7
Amherst Clo. ME16—3F 23
Amherst Redoubt. ME7—6B 4
Amherst Rd. ME1—1J 7
Amhurst Hill. ME7—5B 4
Amhurst Vs. ME15—4B 26
Amies Ho. ME17—6H 27
Amsbury Rd. ME15 & ME17—6C 26
Anchor Rd. ME1—3H 7
Andover Wlk. ME15—2D 28
Anerley Clo. ME16—7D 20
Anglesey Av. ME15—2J 27
Anglesey Clo. ME5—5C 8
Anglewood Clo. ME5—6K 9
Annie Rd. ME6—7D 12
Annvera Rd. ME7—4D 4
Ansell Av. ME4—2B 8
Anson Clo. ME5—6D 8
Anthony's Way. ME2—2J 3
Appleby Clo. ME1—5J 7
Apple Clo. ME6—7D 12
Appledore Ct. ME16—7C 20
Appledore Rd. ME8—1H 9
Archer Rd. ME5—6C 8
Archibald Ho. ME14—7G 21
Ardenlee Dri. ME14—2K 23
Arden St. ME7—5D 4
Arethusa Rd. ME1—4H 7
Argent Ter. ME5—7A 8
Argyle Clo. ME1—4K 7
Armstrong Rd. ME15—6J 23
Arnhem Dri. ME5—5A 8
Arran Grn. ME2—5B 2
Arran Rd. ME15—2J 27
Arthur Rd. ME1—1J 7
Arthur Rd. ME4—4A 10
Arundel Clo. ME5—4K 15
Arundel St. ME14—1H 23
Ascot Clo. ME5—3J 15
Ashbee Clo. ME6—6E 12
Ashburnham Rd. ME14—6H 21
Ashby Clo. ME1—1E 12
Ash Clo. ME5—3D 8
Ash Clo. ME20—5J 19
Ash Cres. ME3—2B 2
Ashdown Clo. ME16—4F 23
Ashdowns Cotts. ME15—4B 26
Ashenden Clo. ME7—1H 3
Ashford Rd. ME14—3K 23
Ashford Rd. ME15—3B 24
Ash Gro. ME16—1E 22
Ashley Rd. ME8—2K 9
Ashmead Clo. ME5—2J 15
Ash Rd. ME2—5E 2
Ash Tree La. ME5—2E 8

Ashurst Rd. ME14—2A 24
Aspen Way. ME5—1E 14
Aspian Dri. ME17—5F 27
Asquith Rd. ME8—6K 9
Association Wlk. ME1—5H 7
Astey Ho. ME15—4K 23
Astley St. ME14—3J 23
Aston Clo. ME5—3G 15
Athelstan Rd. ME4—2A 8
Attlee Cotts. ME2—1B 12
Auden Rd. ME20—3E 18
Audley Av. ME7—3F 9
Austen Way. ME20—2D 18
Austin Clo. ME5—2F 9
Autumn Glade. ME5—5K 15
Aveling Ct. ME2—4G 3
Avenue, The. ME20—5J 19
Averenches Rd. ME14—2D 24
Avery Clo. ME15—6H 23
Avery La. ME15 & ME17—2G 29
Aviemore Gdns. ME14—3D 24
Avington Clo. ME15—6H 23
Avocet Wlk. ME5—3J 15
Avondale Rd. ME7—6E 4
Avon Ho. ME15—7C 24
Aylesford Cres. ME8—7J 5

Backfields. ME1—7G 3
Back La. ME15—2G 29
Back La. ME7—6B 28
Back St. ME17—7H 25 to 4J 29
Baden Rd. ME7—4E 4
Bader Cres. ME5—5B 8
Badger Rd. ME5—4J 15
Bailey Dri. ME7—3H 9
Bakenham Ho. ME1—3H 7
Baker St. ME1—4K 13
  (Burham)
Baker St. ME1—1H 7
  (Rochester)
Bakers Wlk. ME1—5H 3
Balfour Rd. ME4—1B 8
Ballard Ind. Centre. ME5—5J 15
Ballard Ind. Pk. ME5—6E 2
Ballens Rd. ME5—2H 15
Balmer Clo. ME8—5A 10
Balmoral Ho. ME15—3D 28
Balmoral Rd. ME7—6D 4
Bangor Rd. ME2—5C 2
Bankside. ME5—4C 8
Banks Rd. ME2—3H 3
Bank St. ME4—1C 8
Bank St. ME14—1H 23
Bankyfields Clo. ME8—3E 10
Banky Meadow. ME16—4B 22
Banning St. ME2—3G 3
Bannister Rd. ME14—7G 21
Barbados Ter. ME14—7G 21
Barberry Av. ME7—7J 7
Bardell Ter. ME1—6J 3
Barfleur Mnr. ME7—5B 4
  (off Middle St.)
Barfreston Clo. ME15—5H 23
Bargrove Rd. ME14—2A 24
Barham Clo. ME15—3C 28
Barker Rd. ME16—4H 23
Barkis Clo. ME1—5J 7
Barleycorn. ME19—5C 18

Barleycorn Dri. ME8—6B 10
Barleyfields. ME14—3B 24
Barleymow Clo. ME5—5D 8
Barming Pl. ME16—5B 22
Barnaby Ter. ME1—2H 7
Barncroft Dri. ME7—1B 16
Barned Ct. ME16—5B 22
Barnfield. ME5—4B 8
Barn Hill. ME15—7A 26
Barn Hill Cotts. ME15—5B 26
Barnhurst Rd. ME14—6G 21
Barn Meadow. ME2—1C 12
Barnsole Rd. ME7—6E 4
Barnwood Clo. ME1—4G 7
Baron Clo. ME7—4F 5
Barrack Rd. ME3—3C 4
Barrie Dri. ME20—2D 18
Barrier Rd. ME4—6A 4
Barrington Clo. ME5—7A 8
Barrow Clo. ME8—7B 10
Bartlett Clo. ME5—4J 15
Barton Rd. ME2—4F 3
Barton Rd. ME15—5J 23
Basi Clo. ME2—2H 3
Basing Clo. ME15—4K 23
Basmere Clo. ME14—1A 24
Batchelor St. ME4—7B 4
Bates Clo. ME20—3E 18
Bath Hard. ME1—6J 3
Bayswater Dri. ME8—1G 17
Baywell. ME19—4C 18
Beacon Clo. ME8—5A 10
Beacon Hill. ME5—2D 8
Beacon Rd. ME5—2D 8
Beaconsfield Av. ME7—6H 5
Beaconsfield Rd. ME4—2A 8
Beaconsfield Rd. ME15—5G 23
Beacons, The. ME16—7E 26
Bearsted Clo. ME8—1J 9
Beatty Av. ME7—1G 9
Beatty Rd. ME1—4J 7
Beaufort Rd. ME2—2D 2
Beaufort Wlk. ME15—4C 28
Beaulieu Rise. ME1—7J 7
Beaulieu Wlk. ME16—7C 20
Beaumont Rd. ME16—5D 22
Beauworth Pk. ME15—7C 24
Beckenham Dri. ME16—7D 20
Becksbourne Clo. ME14—6G 21
Beddow Way. ME20—4B 20
Bedford Av. ME8—3A 10
Bedford Pl. ME16—3G 23
Bedgebury Clo. ME14—1A 24
Bedson Wlk. ME8—3E 10
Bedwin Clo. ME1—5J 7
Beech Dri. ME16—2E 22
Beechen Bank Rd. ME5—2G 15
Beeches, The. ME5—1G 15
Beeches, The. ME20—5J 19
Beech Gro. ME3—2A 2
Beeching Rd. ME5—2H 15
Beechings Grn. ME8—1K 9
Beechings Way. ME8—7H 5
Beechmore Dri. ME5—3G 15
Beech Rd. ME2—5E 2
Beech Rd. ME19—7D 18
Beechwood Av. ME5—2E 8
Beechwood Rd. ME16—4B 22

Begonia Av. ME8—2K 9
Beke Rd. ME8—1F 17
Belfast Ho. ME15—1C 28
Belgrave Ho. ME2—4G 3
Belgrave St. ME20—7K 13
Bell Cotts. ME1—1K 11
Bell Cres. ME1—5K 13
Bellgrove St. ME5—5G 15
Bell La. ME1—5K 13
Bell La. ME14—2E 24
Bell La. ME20—4F 19
Bellmeadow. ME15—2C 28
Bell Rd. ME15—2C 28
Belmont Clo. ME16—5B 22
Belmont Rd. ME7—7D 4
Belvedere Ho. ME15—3D 28
 (off Connaught Clo.)
Bendon Way. ME8—4A 10
Benenden Mnr. ME8—1J 9
Benenden Rd. ME7—5C 4
Bennetts Cotts. ME7—5C 16
Bentley Clo. ME5—3K 15
Bentley Clo. ME20—5K 19
Bentlif Clo. ME16—2F 23
Berber Rd. ME2—3G 3
Berengrave La. ME8—3B 10
Beresford Av. ME4—2K 7
Beresford Rd. ME7—7E 4
Beresford Rd. ME20—6C 14
Beresfords Hill. ME17—5K 27
Berkeley Clo. ME1—4J 7
Berkshire Clo. ME5—4D 8
Berwyn Gro. ME15—2J 27
Best St. ME4—7A 4
Bethersden Ct. ME15—1D 28
Betjeman Clo. ME20—3D 18
Betsham Rd. ME15—2D 28
Bettescombe Rd. ME8—5A 10
Beverley Clo. ME8—4C 10
Beverley Rd. ME16—5B 22
Bicknor Farm Cotts. ME15—3E 28
Bicknor Rd. ME15—4C 28
Biddenden Clo. ME15—4D 24
Bilsington Clo. ME5—7C 8
Binbury La. ME9—7J 17
Bingdon Rd. ME16—5B 22
Bingham Rd. ME2—2H 3
Bingley Clo. ME6—5D 12
Bingley Rd. ME1—7K 3
Binland Gro. ME5—7J 7
Binnacle Rd. ME1—4H 7
Birch Cres. ME6—6H 19
Birch Dri. ME5—4K 15
Birchfield Clo. ME15—2K 27
Birchfields. ME5—2G 15
Birch Gro. ME7—1C 16
Birchington Clo. ME14—2A 24
Bircholt Rd. ME15—4D 28
Birch Tree Way. ME15—4K 23
Birchwood Rd. ME16—2E 22
Birkhall Clo. ME5—7B 8
Birling Av. ME8—3A 10
Birling Av. ME14—3D 24
Birling Clo. ME14—3D 24
Birling Hill. ME6—4A 12
Birling Pk. Est. ME19—7A 12
Birling Rd. ME6—5D 12
Birling Rd. ME19—5A 18
Birling Rookery Rd. ME6—6D 12
Birnam Sq. ME16—3G 23
Bishopbourne Grn. ME8—7J 5
Bishop La. ME9—1H 11
Bishopsway. ME15—3H 23
Black Cotts. ME14—1K 21
Blacklands. ME19—7D 18
Blackmanstone Way. ME16
—7B 20
Blacksmith Dri. ME14—2B 24
Blackthorn Av. ME5—2G 15
Blackthorn Dri. ME20—4F 19
Blackthorne Rd. ME8—4E 10
Blake Dri. ME20—2D 18
Blaker Av. ME1—3K 7
Blatchford Clo. ME19—5D 18
Bleakwood Rd. ME6—7A 8
Blean Rd. ME8—2K 9
Blean Sq. ME14—1A 24
Blendon Rd. ME14—2A 24
Blenheim Av. ME4—2K 7
Blenheim Clo. ME15—4D 24
Bligh Way. ME2—4B 2
Blind La. ME7—4C 16
Blockmakers Ct. ME4—2C & 3B 8
Bloomsbury Wlk. ME14—3J 23
 (off Wyatt St.)
Bloors La. ME8—3A 10
Blowers Wood Gro. ME7—2D 16
Bluebell Clo. ME7—5G 5
Blue Bell Hill By-Pass. ME5—4C 14
Blue Boar La. ME1—6J 3
Bluett St. ME14—2J 23
Blythe Rd. ME15—3K 23

Boarley Ct. ME14—5F 21
Boarley La. ME14—5F 21
Boarley Rd. ME14—5F 21
Bockingford Clo. ME15—7H 23
Bockingford Ho. ME15—7H 23
Bockingford La. ME15—7H 23
Bodiam Clo. ME8—1K 9
Bodsham Cres. ME15—4F 25
Boiler Rd. ME4—3B 4
Boley Hill. ME1—5H 3
Bolner Clo. ME5—3F 15
Bombay Ho. ME15—3C 28
Bondfield Rd. ME19—6D 18
Bonnington Rd. ME14—1A 24
Bootham Clo. ME2—6C 2
Booth Rd. ME4—2A 8
Borough Rd. ME7—7E 4
Borstal M. ME1—2F 7
Borstal Rd. ME1—1G 7
Borstal St. ME1—2F 7
Boston Rd. ME5—3J 15
Bottlescrew Hill. ME17—4K 27
Boughton Clo. ME8—1K 9
Boughton La. ME15—1K 27
Boughton Pde. ME15—1J 27
Boundary Rd. ME4—1J 7
Bounds, The. ME20—5J 19
Bournewood Clo. ME15—6D 24
Bournville Av. ME4—3A 8
Bower Clo. ME16—3G 23
Bower Grn. ME5—4J 15
Bower Mt. Rd. ME16—4G 23
Bower Mt. Rd. ME16—7B 23
Bower Pl. ME16—4G 23
Bower St. ME16—3G 23
Bower Ter. ME16—4G 23
Bowes Rd. ME2—3G 3
Bowman Clo. ME5—7D 8
Boxgrove Ri. ME14—5F 21
Boxley Clo. ME14—6H 21
Boxley Rd. ME5—3G 15
Boxley Rd. ME14—1J 23 to 4J 21
Brabourne Av. ME8—7K 5
Brackley Clo. ME14—2A 24
Brackwood Clo. ME8—7A 10
Bradbourne La. ME20—5F 19
Braddick Clo. ME15—2K 27
Bradfields Av. ME5—6A 8
Bradfields Av. W. ME5—6A 8
Bradley Rd. ME2—1C 12
Bradshaw Clo. ME9—1H 11
Braes, The. ME3—2B 2
Brake Av. ME5—7K 7
Bramble Clo. ME16—4D 22
Brambledown. ME5—4C 8
Brambletree Cotts. ME1—2D 6
Brambletree Cres. ME1—2E 6
Bramley Clo. ME8—4E 10
Bramley Gro. ME9—7K 11
Bramley Cres. ME15—4D 24
Bramley Rise. ME2—3D 2
Bramley Rd. ME6—5E 12
Bramshott Clo. ME16—1E 22
Bransgore Clo. ME8—5A 10
Brasenose Rd. ME7—1F 9
Brassey Dri. ME20—6H 19
Bray Gdns. ME15—3H 27
Breach La. ME9—5J 11
Bredgar Clo. ME14—2K 23
Bredhurst Rd. ME8—6J 9
Brenchley Clo. ME1—2J 7
Brenchley Ho. ME14—2H 23
Brenchley Rd. ME8—2J 9
Brenchley Rd. ME15—5H 23
Brendon Av. ME15—1G 8
Brent Clo. ME5—7K 7
Brenzett Clo. ME5—7C 8
Breton Rd. ME1—2H 7
Brett Wlk. ME8—1F 17
Brewer St. ME14—2J 23
Briar Clo. ME20—4E 18
Briar Dale. ME3—1A 2
Brice Rd. ME3—2A 2
Bridge Cotts. ME15—1C 26
Bridge Cotts. ME16—7A 22
Bridge Mill Way. ME15—5F 23
Bridge Rd. ME1—2H 7
Bridge Rd. ME7—4D 4
Bridge St. ME15—3H 27
Bridgewater Pl. ME19—4C 18
Brier Clo. ME8—6D 8
Bright Rd. ME4—2D 8
Brindle Way. ME5—4J 15
Brisbane Rd. ME4—1B 8
Brishing Clo. ME15—3C 28
Brishing La. ME17 & ME15—6B 28
Brishing Rd. ME17—4C 28
Brissenden Clo. ME2—1B 4
Bristol Clo. ME2—6C 2
Bristol Ho. ME15—1B 28
Britannia Clo. ME2—1E 12
Britton Farm Rd. ME7—5D 4

Britton St. ME7—6C 4
Broadfield Rd. ME15—7J 23
Broadlands Dri. ME5—1H 15
Broadoak. ME19—4B 18
Broadoak Av. ME15—7J 23
Broadview Av. ME8—4B 10
Broadwater Rd. ME19—7C 18
Broadway. ME8—1H 9
Broadway. ME16—4H 23
Broadway Shopping Centre. ME16
—3H 23
Brockenhurst Av. ME15—6K 23
Brockenhurst Clo. ME8—5K 9
 (in two parts)
Bromley Clo. ME5—1H 15
Brompton Clo. ME4—5A 4
Brompton Farm Rd. ME2
—2E 2 to 1G 3
Brompton Hill. ME4—5A 4
Brompton La. ME2—3F 3
Brompton Rd. ME7—5C 4
Bronington Clo. ME5—7B 8
Bronte Clo. ME20—3D 18
Brookbank. ME14—6G 21
Brookfield Av. ME20—2E 18
Brooklands Rd. ME20—2E 18
Brook La. ME6—7D 12
Brooklyn Paddock. ME7—5E 4
Brook Rd. ME20—2D 18
Brooks Pl. ME14—3J 23
Brook St. ME6—5F 13
Brook, The. ME4—6A 4
Broomcroft Rd. ME8—2C 10
Broom Hill Rd. ME2—3E 2
Broomshaw Rd. ME16—4B 22
Browndens Rd. ME2—1C 12
Brownelow Copse. ME5—4G 15
Browning Clo. ME20—2D 18
Brown St. ME8—3B 10
Brunswick St. ME15—4J 23
Brunswick St. E. ME15—4J 23
Bryant Rd. ME2—3F 3
Bryant St. ME4—1A 8
Buckingham Rd. ME7—6E 4
Buckingham Row. ME15—1C 28
Buckland Clo. ME5—3G 15
Buckland Hill. ME16—2G 23
Buckland La. ME16—1F 23
Buckland Rd. ME16—2G 23
Buffalo Cotts. ME17—7F 29
 (off Amber La.)
Buglehorn Cotts. ME15—2G 28
Bulldog Rd. ME5—3H 15
Buller Rd. ME4—2A 8
Bull Fields. ME6—5E 12
Bull La. ME7—1K 11
Bull La. ME9—7K 11
Bull La. ME19—1A 18
Bull La. ME20—3K 19 to 6A 14
Bull Orchard. ME16—5B 22
Bulrush Clo. ME5—2F 15
Bulrushes, The. ME6—6E 12
Bumbles Clo. ME1—4J 7
Burberry La. ME7—4K 29
Burgess Cotts. ME17—3K 29
Burgess Rd. ME2—4G 3
Burghclere Dri. ME16—5D 22
Burgoyne Ct. ME14—7F 21
Burham Rd. ME1—5D 6
Burleigh Clo. ME2—3D 2
Burlington Gdns. ME8—1G 17
Burmarsh Clo. ME5—7C 8
Burma Way. ME5—6A 8
Burnham Wlk. ME8—2G 17
Burn Meadow Cotts. ME14—3J 21
Burns Rd. ME7—4D 4
Burns Rd. ME16—5E 22
Burntash Rd. ME20—6K 19
Burnt Ho. Clo. ME3—1H 3
Burnt Oak Ter. ME7—5D 4
Burritt St. ME1—1H 7
Burston Rd. ME17—6D 26
Busbridge Rd. ME6—6C 12
Busbridge Rd. ME15—2G 27
Bushmeadow Rd. ME8—2C 10
Bush Rd. ME2—1A 6
Bush Row. ME20—3A 20
Buttermere Clo. ME7—6G 5
Button La. ME15—5F 25
Buxton Clo. ME5—4K 15
Buxton Clo. ME15—7J 23
Bychurch Pl. ME15—4J 23
Byron Rd. ME7—1D 8
Byron Way. ME14—7H 21

Cadet Clo. ME7—3H 9
Cadnam Clo. ME2—3D 2
Caernavon Dri. ME15—6H 23
Cagetown Ter. ME14—7G 21
Calcutta Ho. ME15—3C 28
Calden Av. ME8—3K 9
Calder Rd. ME14—7E 20

Caledonian Ct. ME8—4B 10
Calehill Clo. ME14—1A 24
Callams Clo. ME8—6A 10
Callaways La. ME9—6K 11
Callis Way. ME8—7A 10
Cambria Av. ME1—2E 6
Cambridge Cres. ME15—1B 28
Cambridge Ho. ME15—1B 28
Cambridge Rd. ME2—3F 3
Cambridge Rd. ME8—6K 9
Cambridge Ter. ME4—7A 4
Camden Clo. ME5—7C 8
Camden St. ME14—2J 23
Camder Rd. ME7—4E 4
Camellia Clo. ME5—5A 10
Cameron Clo. ME5—4C 8
Campbell Rd. ME15—4J 23
Campion Clo. ME5—2E 14
Campleshon Rd. ME8—7A 10
Camp Way. ME15—1A 28
Canada Ter. ME14—7G 21
Canadian Av. ME7—7F 5
Canal Rd. ME2—4H 3
Canning St. ME14—1J 23
Canon Clo. ME1—2G 7
Canterbury Ho. ME15—1B 28
 (off Cambridge Cres.)
Canterbury La. ME8 & ME9—2F 11
Canterbury St. ME7—6D 4
Capel Clo. ME8—7A 10
Capell Clo. ME17—5E 26
Capetown Ho. ME15—3D 28
Capstone Rd. ME8—3D 8
Caring La. ME17—6H 25
Caring Rd. ME15 & ME17—5G 25
Carisbrooke Dri. ME16—2F 23
Carisbrooke Rd. ME2—2D 2
Carlisle Clo. ME2—5B 2
Carlisle Ho. ME15—1B 28
 (off Nottingham Av.)
Carlton Av. ME7—7F 5
Carlton Cres. ME5—4E 8
Carlton Gdns. ME15—7J 23
Carnation Cres. ME19—5E 18
Carnation Cres. ME19—6D 18
Carnation Dri. ME4—2C 2
Carnation Rd. ME2—4C 2
Caroline Gdns. ME16—7D 20
Carpeaux Clo. ME4—7B 4
Carroll Gdns. ME20—3D 18
Carton Clo. ME1—2J 7
Carton Rd. ME3—2A 2
Carvoran Way. ME8—7K 9
Castle Av. ME1—7H 3
Castle Dene. ME14—6F 21
Castle Hill. ME1—5H 3
Castlemaine Av. ME7—5G 5
Castle Rd. ME4—2B 8
Castle Rd. ME16—6D & 7E 20
Castle St. ME1—1G 13
Castle St. ME2—2K 3
Castle View Rd. ME2—4F 3
Catherine St. ME1—1J 7
Catkin Clo. ME5—4F 15
Catlyn Clo. ME19—6E 18
Catterick Rd. ME5—3K 15
Cave Hill. ME15—6G 23
Cavendish Av. ME7—5F 5
Cavendish Rd. ME1—1J 7
Cavendish Way. ME15—4E 24
Cazeneuve St. ME1—6H 3
Cecil Av. ME2—3G 3
Cecil Av. ME8—2H 9
Cecil Rd. ME1—1H 7
Cedar Clo. ME20—6H 19
Cedar Ct. ME14—2K 23
Cedar Dri. ME16—5A 22
Cedar Gro. ME7—7H 9
Cedar Rd. ME2—5D 2
Celestine Clo. ME5—4G 15
Cemetery Cotts. ME15—1A 28
Cemetery Rd. ME2—1E 12
Cemetery Rd. ME6—4D 12
Central Av. ME4—4C 4
Central Pde. ME1—2J 7
Central Pk. Gdns. ME4—2K 7
Central Rd. ME2—4F 3
Central Rd. ME20—3F 19
Century Building. ME1—6H 3
Century Rd. ME8—4A 10
Chada Av. ME7—1F 9
Chaffe's La. ME9—2H 11
Chaffinch Clo. ME5—5B 8
Chalfont Rd. ME8—6A 10
Chalkenden Av. ME8—2H 9
Chalk Pit Hill. ME4—1B 8
Chalky Bank Rd. ME8—2C 10
Challock Wlk. ME14—1A 24
Chamberlain Av. ME16—5D 22
Chamberlain Rd. ME4—2C 8
Chancery La. ME15—3J 23

Chapel La. ME7—1C & 2C 16
Chapel La. ME14—2E 24
Chapel La. ME15—4D 26
Chapel Rd. ME6—5E 12
Chapel St. ME19—7E 18
Chapman Av. ME15—6C 24
Chapman Way. ME19—6D 18
Chapter Rd. ME2—4E 2
Chard Ho. ME14—7F 21
Charing Rd. ME8—1J 9
Charlbury Clo. ME16—4E 22
Charlecote Ct. ME4—4A 10
(off Derwent Way.)
Charles Busby Ct. ME20—5K 19
Charles Clo. ME6—5E 12
Charles Dickens Av. ME3—3B 2
Charles Dri. ME2—1A 6
Charles St. ME2—4F 3
Charles St. ME4—1K 7
Charles St. ME15—4G 23
Charlton La. ME15—1A 26
Charlton Mnr. ME7—6D 4
Charlton St. ME16—5E 22
Chart Corner Cotts. ME17—7F 29
(off Amber La.)
Charter St. ME4—2A & 1A 8
(in two parts)
Chart Hill Rd. ME17—7F 29
Chart Pl. ME8—2E 16
Chartway St. ME17—7J 29
Chartwell Clo. ME2—2G 3
Chase, The. ME4—2J 7
Chase, The. ME8—2H 9
Chatham Gro. ME4—3A 8
Chatham Hill. ME5—1C 8
Chatham Rd. ME20—5D 14 to 1E 20
Chatsworth Dri. ME2—2G 3
Chatsworth Rd. ME7—5D 4
Chattenden Ct. ME14—7H 21
Chaucer Clo. ME15—1C 28
Chaucer Rd. ME7—1E 8
Chaucer Way. ME20—2D 18
Chaulkers Ho. ME4—2C 8
(off Shipwright Av.)
Chegwell Dri. ME5—1H 15
Chelmar Rd. ME4—7C 4
Chelmsford Ho. ME15—2C 28
Chelmsford Rd. ME2—5C 2
Chelsfield Ho. ME16—2F 23
Cheney Clo. ME8—7A 10
Chequers Shopping Centre. ME15
—3J 23
Cherbourg Cres. ME5—5A 8
Cheriton Rd. ME8—5A 10
Cheriton Way. ME16—7C 20
Cherries, The. ME16—5C 22
Cherry Amber Clo. ME8—4C 10
Cherry Orchard. ME20—6G 19
Cherry Orchard Way. ME16—4D 22
Cherry Tree Rd. ME8—4C 10
Chervilles. ME16—5C 22
Chesham Dri. ME8—6B 10
Cheshire Av. ME15—4C 24
Cheshire Rd. ME15—1C 28
Chester Clo. ME2—5C 2
Chesterfield Clo. ME8—2B 10
Chester Rd. ME2—2E 8
Chesterton Rd. ME20—2D 18
Chestnut Av. ME5—2E 14
Chestnut Clo. ME17—5D 26
Chestnut Rd. ME2—5D 2
Chestnut Wlk. ME20—4F 19
Chetney Clo. ME2—4B 2
Chevening Clo. ME5—7B 8
Cheviot Gdns. ME15—6E 24
Chicago Av. ME7—6F 5
Chichester Clo. ME8—4D 10
Chichester Ho. ME15—1B 28
Chickfield Gdns. ME5—2D 8
Chiddingstone Clo. ME15—2D 28
Chieftain Clo. ME7—3J 9
Childscroft Rd. ME8—2C 10
Chilham Ho. ME2—2H 3
(off Cypress Rd.)
Chilham Rd. ME8—1H 9
Chilham Rd. ME16—7C 20
Chilington Clo. ME2—1C 12
Chillington St. ME14—1H 23
Chilton Ct. ME8—3B 10
Chilton Dri. ME3—2A 2
Chippendale Clo. ME5—4F 15
Chipstead Clo. ME16—1F 23
Chipstead Rd. ME2—1F 17
Chislehurst Clo. ME15—2D 28
Chislet Wlk. ME8—1F 17
Chrismill Cotts. ME14—4J 25
Chrismill La. ME14—4J 25
Christchurch Ct. ME4—2B 8
Christen Way. ME17—5D 28
Christie Dri. ME20—2D 18
Christmas St. ME7—4F 5

Church Farm Rd. ME9—1H 11
Church Field. ME6—4F 13
Church Fields. ME19—6A 18
Churchfields Ter. ME1—7G 3
Church Grn. ME2—3H 3
Church Hill. ME5—2D 8
Church Hill. ME17—7A 28
Churchill Av. ME5—6A 8
Churchill Ho. ME16—5D 22
Churchlands. ME3—3A 8
Church La. ME4—5A 4
Church La. ME14—3G 25
Church La. ME17—6K 27
Church M. ME8—4C 10
Church Pde. ME2—4G 3
Church Path. ME7—5E 4
Church Rd. ME15—5G 23
(Maidstone)
Church Rd. ME15—1D 28
(Otham)
Church St. ME1—5J 13
(Burham)
Church St. ME1—7J 3
(Rochester)
Church St. ME4—7B 4
Church St. ME7—5F 5
Church St. ME14—3J 23
Church St. ME15—3H 27
(Loose)
Church St. ME15—5G 23
(Tovil)
Church St. ME17—5K 27
Church Ter. ME5—2D 8
Church Wlk. ME19—7E 18
Chute Clo. ME8—1F 17
Cinnabar Clo. ME5—4G 15
City Way. ME1—7J 3
Clandon Rd. ME5—3K 15
Clare La. ME19—6C 18
Claremont Rd. ME14—2K 23
Claremont Way. ME14—1A 8
Clarence Av. ME1—7H 3
Clarence Ct. ME14—3C 24
Clarence Rd. ME4—2C 8
Clarendon Clo. ME14—3E 24
Clarendon Pl. ME14—3J 23
(off King St.)
Clark M. ME20—5K 19
Clavell Clo. ME8—1G 17
Claygate. ME15—6B 24
Cleave Rd. ME7—5F 5
Clematis Av. ME8—7J 9
Clement Ct. ME16—2F 23
Clermont Clo. ME2—2C 16
Cleveland Ho. ME16—5D 22
Cleveland Rd. ME7—5E 4
Clewson Rise. ME14—6H 21
Cliffe Rd. ME2—1F 3
Cliff Hill. ME17—4A 28
Cliff Hill Rd. ME17—3K 27
Clifton Clo. ME2—5E 2
Clifton Clo. ME14—2K 23
Clifton Rd. ME7—4D 4
Clinton Av. ME2—3C 2
Clinton Clo. ME17—5D 26
Clive Ho. ME20—6K 19
Clive Rd. ME1—1H 7
Cloisterham Park. ME1—5J 7
Clopton Ct. ME8—4A 10
(off Derwent Way.)
Close, The. ME1—7H 3
Clover St. ME4—7A 4
Cobb Clo. ME2—3C 2
Cobbett Clo. ME16—6D 18
Cobblestones. ME7—7G 9
Cobden Rd. ME4—2C 8
Cobdown Clo. ME20—4F 19
Cobdown Gro. ME8—2D 10
Cobfield. ME17—7E 28
Cobham Clo. ME2—4D 2
Cobham Clo. ME16—3G 23
Cobtree Clo. ME5—4D 8
Cobtree Rd. ME17—5E 26
Colchester Clo. ME5—5A 8
Coldblow Cotts. ME17—6J 27
Coldharbour La. ME20—6A 20
Coldred Rd. ME15—4D 28
Colegate Dri. ME14—3G 25
Coleridge Clo. ME20—2D 18
Coleshill Clo. ME15—2D 28
Colewood Dri. ME2—3A 2
College Av. ME7—7C 4
College Av. ME15—4H 23
College Ct. ME15—4J 23
College Rd. ME4—4A 4
College Rd. ME15—5H 23
College Rd. ME20—3F 19
College Wlk. ME15—4J 23
College Yd. ME1—5H 3
Collet Wlk. ME8—1F 17
Collings Wlk. ME8—1F 17
Collington Ter. ME15—4C 28

Collingwood Rd. ME20—6C 14
Collis St. ME2—3F 3
Colman Ho. ME14—3J 23
(off King St.)
Columbine Clo. ME2—4D 2
Columbine Clo. ME19—5D 18
Columbine Rd. ME2—4D 2
Columbine Rd. ME19—5D 18
Command Rd. ME14—7F 21
Commercial Rd. ME2—4F 3
Commissioners Rd. ME2—3H 3
Commodore Rd. ME14—2A 24
Common Rd. ME5—3A 14
Common, The. ME1—5H 3
Compton Clo. ME5—3K 15
Concord Av. ME5—7K 7
Conifer Dri. ME5—4K 15
Coniston Clo. ME7—5H 5
Coniston Ho. ME15—1C 28
Connaught Clo. ME15—4D 28
Connaught Rd. ME4—2C 8
Connaught Rd. ME7—6E 4
Conrad Clo. ME8—1F 17
Consort Clo. ME14—2K 23
Constitution Hill. ME5—1C 8
Constitution Hill. ME6—5D 12
Constitution Rd. ME5—1C 8
Conway Clo. ME2—2D 2
Conway Rd. ME16—1E 22
Cooden Clo. ME8—2D 10
Cook Clo. ME5—6D 8
Cookham Hill. ME1—2F 7
Cookham Wood Rd. ME1—4G 7
Cooling Clo. ME14—1A 24
Cooling Rd. ME2—1G 3
Coombe Clo. ME5—2H 15
Coombe Rd. ME15—5H 23
Cooper Rd. ME5—2H 15
Cooper Rd. ME6—7D 12
Copenhagen Rd. ME7—6D 4
Copperfield Cres. ME3—3B 2
Copperfield Dri. ME17—4J 29
Copperfield Rd. ME1—2H 7
Coppergate. ME7—6G 9
Copperhouse Rd. ME2—4B 2
Copper Tree Ct. ME15—3J 27
Coppertree Wlk. ME14—4J 15
Coppice Rd. ME5—3J 15
Coppice, The. ME20—5J 19
Copsehill. ME19—4C 18
Copsewood Way. ME15—4E 24
Cordelia Cres. ME1—2E 6
Cork St. ME20—7K 13
Corkwell St. ME4—1K 7
Cormorant Clo. ME2—4B 2
Cornflower Clo. ME14—3C 24
Cornwall Clo. ME15—1C 28
Cornwall Cres. ME1—1H 13
Cornwallis Av. ME4—3K 7
Cornwallis Av. ME7—7G 5
Cornwallis Cotts. ME17—6G 27
Cornwallis Rd. ME16—3F 23
Cornwall Rd. ME1—1H 7
Cornwall Rd. ME7—7G 5
Corona Ter. ME6—7D 12
Coronation Flats. ME4—1A 8
Coronation Rd. ME5—2D 8
Corporation Rd. ME7—5E 4
Corporation St. ME1—5H 3
Corral Clo. ME5—2E 8
Corrance Grn. ME15—7J 23
Cossack St. ME1—1H 7
Cossington Rd. ME5—4H 15
Cotswold Gdns. ME15—6E 24
Cottage Rd. ME4—5A 4
Cottall Av. ME4—2A 8
Cottenham Clo. ME19—7D 18
Coulman St. ME7—6E 4
Coulters Clo. ME14—3B 24
Council Cotts. ME15—4C 26
County Gro. ME19—6A 18
County Rd. ME14—2J 23
Court Dri. ME16—3F 23
Courtenay Rd. ME15—5H 23
Courtenay Rd. ME8—5J 9
Courtfield Av. ME5—3H 15
Court La. Cotts. ME15—1C 26
Court Lodge Rd. ME7—5G 5
Court Rd. ME1—5K 13
Court Rd. ME8—4D 10
Coventry Clo. ME2—5C 2
Coventry Ho. ME15—1B 28
Coverdale Av. ME15—2B 28
Coverdale Clo. ME5—5C 8
Covert, The. ME2—4A 2
Covey Hall Rd. ME6—4E 12
Cowbeck Clo. ME8—6A 10
Cowden Rd. ME14—2A 24
Cowdrey Clo. ME1—2G 7
Cowdrey Clo. ME16—5D 22
Cowper Rd. ME7—1E 8
Cox's Clo. ME6—5D 12

Cox St. ME9—7F 17
Coyers Ct. .ME8—1F 17
Cozenton Clo. ME8—3B 10
Crabtree Rd. ME8—4A 10
Craddock Way. ME8—7A 10
Cradles Rd. ME9—3K 17
Cranborne Av. ME15—7K 23
Cranbrook Clo. ME8—1K 9
Cranbrook Clo. ME15—1D 28
Crane Rd. ME4—3B 4
Cranford Clo. ME8—3A 10
Cranleigh Gdns. ME4—1J 7
Cranleigh Gdns. ME16—7C 20
Crayford Clo. ME14—1A 24
Crescent, The. ME14—6F 21
Crescent, The. ME20—6K 19
Crescent Way. ME5—7J 7
Cressy Ct. ME4—7K 3
Crest Rd. ME1—3H 7
Crestway. ME5—4C 8
Creve Couer Clo. ME14—2E 24
Cripple St. ME15—7H 23
Crispe Clo. ME8—1F 17
Crispin Rd. ME2—3D 2
Crittenden Cotts. ME15—4B 26
Croft Clo. ME5—4J 15
Croft, The. ME4—4C 18
Cromer Rd. ME2—3G 3
Cromwell Rd. ME14—2J 23
Cromwell Ter. ME4—1B 8
Cronin Clo. ME20—2D 18
Crosier Ct. ME9—1H 11
Crosley Rd. ME7—1E 8
Crossfield Pavilion. ME20—6K 19
Cross Keys. ME14—3G 25
Cross Keys Cotts. ME14—3G 25
Cross St. ME2—3G 3
Cross St. ME4—7B 4
Cross St. ME7—5D 4
Cross St. ME14—1J 23
Cross Way. ME1—1H 7
Crossway. ME5—6K 7
Crossways. ME17—7F 29
(off Amber La.)
Crow La. ME1—6H 3
Crown Ho. ME14—2K 23
Crown St. ME7—5E 4
Croydon Clo. ME5—1J 15
Crundale. ME14—2J 23
Crundale Rd. ME8—1K 9
Crusader Clo. ME8—4J 9
Crutches La. ME3 & ME2—3A 2
Cuckmere Ho. ME15—7C 24
Cudham Clo. ME14—1A 24
Culpepper Clo. ME8—1F 17
Culpepper Rd. ME17—5D 26
Cumberland Av. ME15—7B 24
Cumberland Rd. ME4—4B 4
Cunningham Cres. ME5—4B 8
Curlew Av. ME9—1K 11
Curlew Cres. ME2—5B 2
Curzon Rd. ME4—1A 8
Curzon Rd. ME14—1J 23
Cutbush Almshouses. ME15
—4H 23
Cut, The. ME4—5A 4
Cuxton Rd. ME2—7D 2
Cuxton Rd. ME15—3D 28
Cygnet Clo. ME20—4E 18
Cygnet Rd. ME5—3J 15
Cypress Rd. ME2—3H 3

Daffodil Rd. ME2—4D 2
Dagmar Rd. ME4—2C 8
Dale Rd. ME1—1H 7
Dale St. ME4—2K 7
Dalton St. ME7—5D 4
Damien St. ME8—2B 8
Dane Clo. ME5—3J 15
Dane Clo. ME9—7G 11
Dane Ct. ME17—6E 26
Danefield Ct. ME14—3F 25
Dane La. ME9—7G 11
Danes Hill. ME5—5H 5
Danson Way. ME8—3A 10
Darenth Ho. ME15—7B 24
Darenth Rise. ME5—2H 15
Dargate Clo. ME16—7D 20
Dargets Rd. ME5—2G 15
Darland Av. ME7—2F 9
Darnley Clo. ME2—5C 2
Darnley Rd. ME2—5C 2
Dart Clo. ME2—5E 2
Dashmonden Clo. ME2—1H 3
Davenport Av. ME7—5F 5
Dawes St. ME7—6D 4
Dawson Cotts. ME15—2A 26
Dawson Ho. ME14—7G 21
Deacon Clo. ME15—4J 15
Dean Rd. ME2—3E 2
Dean St. ME15—4C 26
Deanwood Clo. ME8—6A 10

Deanwood Dri. ME8
　　　　—3E 16 to 6A 10
Defiant Clo. ME5—6C 8
Delamere Gdns. ME6—5E 12
Delamere Rd ME6—5F 13
Delce Rd. ME1—7J 3
Delting Ho. ME8—2K 9
De Mere Clo. ME8—6A 10
Denbigh Av. ME8—3A 10
Dennis Cadman Ho. ME20—5K 19
Denstead Wlk. ME15—2D 28
Denton Clo. ME5—7C 24
Denton Grn. ME8—7J 5
Derby Rd. ME5—2F 9
Derby Rd. ME15—7A 24
Deringwood Dri. ME15—5D 24
Derwent Ho. ME1—1C 28
Derwent Way. ME8—4A 10
Devon Clo. ME5—5D 8
Devon Clo. ME8—3C 10
Devon Rd. ME15—7A 24
Devonshire Rd. ME7—4E 4
Dhekelia Clo. ME14—7G 21
Dial Rd. ME7—5G 5
Dickens Clo. ME17—4J 29
Dickens Dri. ME19—5D 18
Dickens Rd. ME1—2H 7
Dickens Rd. ME14—7E 20
Dignals Clo. ME8—2C 10
Dillywood La. ME3—1D 2
Disraeli Clo. ME15—3C 28
Ditton Ct. Clo. ME20—5F 19
Ditton Pl. ME20—5G 19
Dixon Clo. ME15—5H 23
Dixwell Clo. ME8—7A 10
Dock Head Rd. ME4—2B 4
Dock Rd. ME4—6A 4
Doddington Clo. ME16—2G 23
Doddington Rd. ME8—1A 10
Doggett's Sq. ME2—4G 3
Dogwood Clo. ME5—4K 15
Dolphin Dri. ME8—7B 10
Dombey Clo. ME1—1H 7
Dombey Clo. ME3—2B 2
Donega Rd. ME2—2G 3
Donet Clo. ME8—7A 10
Dornden Gdns. ME5—3H 15
Dorrit Way. ME1—2J 7
Dorset Sq. ME8—3A 10
Dorset Way. ME15—7A 24
Dotterel Clo. ME5—3K 15
Douglas Rd. ME16—4G 23
Dove Clo. ME5—6C 8
Dover Ho. ME2—2H 3
(off Cypress Rd.)
Dover La. ME15—5E 22
Downderry Way. ME20—5F 19
Downs Clo. ME14—6H 21
Downside. ME4—4F 3
Downs Rd. ME14—6H 21
Downs, The. ME20—4D 14
Downs View. ME1—4K 13
Downs View. ME4—4C 8
Downs View Rd. ME14—6G 21
Drake's Av. ME2—3E 2
Drakes Clo. ME9—2H 11
Drewery Dri. ME8—7K 9
Drylands Rd. ME6—6D 12
Dublin Ho. ME15—1C 28
Duchess Clo. ME2—3D 2
Duchess of Kent Ct. ME20—5J 19
Duchess of Kent Dri. ME5—2H 15
Dukes Meadow Dri. ME7—6G 9
Dukes Wlk. ME15—3J 23
Duncan Rd. ME7—6F 5
Dundas Ho. ME14—7F 21
Dunera Grn. ME14—7F 21
Dunkeld Ho. ME15—1C 28
Dunkirk Clo. ME5—6A 8
Dunning's La. ME1—7H 3
Dunnis Clo. ME8—1F 17
Dunn St. Rd. ME7—6B 16
Durban Ho. ME15—3C 28
(off Bell Rd.)
Durham Clo. ME15—6C 24
Durham Rd. ME8—5K 9
Durling Ct. ME8—3D 10
Durrant Ho. ME14—7G 21
Duval Dri. ME1—4K 7

Eagle Clo. ME20—4E 18
Eagle Ct. ME1—6H 3
Ealing Clo. ME5—1H 15
Earl Gro. ME15—1H 15
Earl St. ME14—3H 23
Eastcourt Grn. ME8—1J 9
Eastcourt La. ME8 & ME7
　　　　—6K & 7J 5
(in two parts)
Eastern Rd. ME7—5G 5
Eastfield Ho. ME16—5D 22
Eastgate. ME1—6J 3
Eastgate Ct. ME1—6H 3

Eastgate Ter. ME1—6H 3
East Hill. ME5—3E 8
Eastling Clo. ME8—1A 10
E. Park Rd. ME20—5A 20
East Rd. ME4—3B 4
E. Row. ME1—6H 3
Eastry Clo. ME16—7C 20
East St. ME4—1B 8
East St. ME5—5F 13
East St. ME7—5E 4
East St. ME15—7B 26
Eastwell Clo. ME14—2A 24
Eccles Row. ME20—7K 13
Eccleston Rd. ME15—5H 23
Echo Clo. ME17—2D 28
Eddington Clo. ME15—2K 27
Eden Av. ME5—5A 8
Edinburgh Rd. ME4—2D 8
Edinburgh Rd. ME7—6E 4
Edinburgh Sq. ME15—1A 28
Edisbury Wlk. ME8—7A 10
Edna Rd. ME14—7F 21
Edwards Clo. ME8—7K 9
Edward St. ME4—1B 8
Edward Wlk. ME14—7F 21
Edwin Rd. ME8—4J 9
Egerton Rd. ME14—7E 20
Egremont Rd. ME15—5D 24
Egypt Pl. ME14—3G 25
(off Street, The.)
Elaine Av. ME2—5D 2
Elaine Ct. ME2—5D 2
Elbon St. ME4—7B 4
Elgin Gdns. ME2—6C 2
Elham Clo. ME8—2J 9
Eling Ct. ME15—7J 23
Elizabeth Clo. ME14—3J 23
Elizabeth Ho. ME14—1J 23
(off Alexandra St.)
Ellenswood Clo. ME15—6D 24
Ellingham Leas. ME15—1A 28
Ellison Way. ME8—2D 10
Elm Av. ME4—3K 7
Elm Clo. ME3—2B 2
Elm Cres. ME19—6D 18
Elmfield. ME8—1H 9
Elm Gro. ME15—4K 23
Elmhurst Gdns. ME4—1J 7
Elm Rd. ME7—5F 5
Elmstone Clo. ME16—5D 22
Elmstone La. ME16—5C 22
Elmstone Rd. ME8—5A 10
Elm Tree Dri. ME1—2F 7
Elm Wlk. ME20—5J 19
Elphinstone Ho. ME14—7F 21
Elvington Clo. ME16—2F 23
Ely Clo. ME8—2B 10
Ely Ho. ME15—1B 28
(off Leicester Rd.)
Embassy Ct. ME7—3G 9
Emerald Clo. ME7—5J 7
Emsworth Gro. ME14—1B 24
Ennerdale Rd. ME15—1C 28
Enterprise Centre, The. ME5—5J 15
Enterprise Clo. ME2—3J 3
Epaul La. ME1—5H 3
Erith La. ME14—6G 21
Ernest Dri. ME16—2D 22
Ernest Rd. ME1—4B 8
Esplanade. ME1—1F 7 to 5H 3
Esplanade. ME2—5G 3
Essex Rd. ME2—3B 12
Essex La. ME15—2C 28
Essie Harris Pavilion. ME20
　　　　—6K 19
Estelle Clo. ME1—5J 7
Ethelbert Rd. ME1—7H 3
Eton Clo. ME5—1F 15
Eva Rd. ME7—1E 8
Evelyn Rd. ME16—4G 23
Everest La. ME2—2G 3
Everglades, The. ME7—6G 9
Evergreen Clo. ME3—2A 2
Evergreen Clo. ME7—7H 9
Evergreen Clo. ME19—4C 18
Eversley Clo. ME16—7C 20
Ewart Rd. ME4—3K 7
Ewell La. ME15—3A 26
Exeter Ho. ME15—1B 28
Exeter Wlk. ME1—5H 7
Exmouth Rd. ME7—4D 4
Exton Clo. ME5—3J 15
Eynsford Rd. ME16—7D 20

Factory Cotts. ME2—1C 6
Fairfax Clo. ME8—7A 10
Fairfax Ho. ME15—3C 28
Fairlead Rd. ME1—3J 7
Fairmeadow. ME14—3H 23
Fairview Av. ME8—7J 9
Fairview Cotts. ME15—2A 26

Fairview Dri. ME3—1A 2
Fairway. ME1—3H 7
Fairway, The. ME1—3H 7
Falcon Grn. ME20—5D 18
Falkland Pl. ME5—4E 14
Fallowfield. ME5—4C 8
Fanconi Rd. ME5—2H 15
Fancy Row. ME14—2G 25
Fane Way. ME8—1E 16
Fant La. ME16—5D 22
Faraday Clo. ME1—4J 7
Faraday Rd. ME14—7J 21
Fareham Wlk. ME15—2D 28
Farleigh Clo. ME16—5C 22
Farleigh Hill. ME15—7F 23
Farleigh La. ME16—5C 22
Farley Clo. ME5—3K 15
Farm Cotts. ME15—6B 24
Farmdale Av. ME1—2E 6
Farmer Clo. ME17—2K 29
Farm Hill Av. ME2—2E 2
Farm Rd. ME5—2E 14
Farnborough Clo. ME16—5E 22
Farne Clo. ME15—2J 27
Farnham Clo. ME8—3E 10
Farningham Clo. ME14—1A 24
Farrier Clo. ME14—2C 24
Farthings Cotts. ME14—5F 21
Fatham Ho. ME1—3H 7
Fauchon's Clo. ME14—4D 24
Fauchon's La. ME14—4D 24
Fawley Clo. ME14—7E 20
Featherby Rd. ME8—2H 9 to 6K 5
(in two parts)
Felderland Clo. ME17—3B 28
Felderland Dri. ME15—3C 28
Felderland Rd. ME15—3C 28
Feldspar Clo. ME5—4F 15
Fernbank Clo. ME5—3E 14
Ferndale Rd. ME7—6F 5
Ferndown Clo. ME7—7H 9
Fern Hill Rd. ME16—5C 22
Fernleigh Rise. ME20—4F 19
Ferns, The. ME20—4F 19
Ferry La. ME1—1G 13
Ferry Rd. ME2—1F 13
Ffinch Clo. ME20—6H 19
Field Clo. ME5—6K 7
Field Clo. ME15—1D 28
Fielding Dri. ME20—3E 18
Fieldworks Rd. ME4—4B 4
Finch Ct. ME14—7E 20
Findley Ho. ME14—7F 21
Fintonagh Dri. ME14—7H 21
Finwell Rd. ME8—2D 10
Firethorn Clo. ME7—5G 5
Firs Clo. ME20—5J 19
Firs La. ME17—5J 25
First Av. ME4—2D 8
First Av. ME7—2F 9
Fir Tree Gro. ME5—4K 15
Fir Tree Gro. ME7—4D 16
Fisher Rd. ME5—5C 8
Fisher St. ME14—1J 23
Fitzwilliam Rd. ME14—2D 24
Flamingo Clo. ME5—5B 8
Flaxman Dri. ME16—1E 22
Flaxmans Ct. ME7—5B 4
Fleet Rd. ME1—5J 7
Flint Grn. ME5—2J 15
Flood Hatch. ME15—5F 23
Florence Rd. ME16—4G 23
Florence St. ME2—3G 3
Foley St. ME14—2J 23
Foord St. ME1—7H 3
Fordcombe Clo. ME15—1D 28
Fordwich Clo. ME16—7B 20
Foremans Barn Rd. ME15—5B 26
Forestdale Rd. ME5—5G 15
Forest Dri. ME5—3F 15
Foresters Clo. ME5—3F 15
Forest Hill. ME15—6H 23
Forge Bungalows. ME15—6B 24
Forge Cotts. ME14—3G 25
(off Green, The.)
Forge Clo. ME17—5K 27
Forge La. ME4—4C 16
Forge La. ME3—3B 2
Forge La. ME4—4C 16
(Bredhurst)
Forge La. ME7—5F 5
(Gillingham)
Forge La. ME9—1H 11
Forge La. ME14—4J 21
Forge La. ME15—1D 26
Forge La. ME17—1J 29
Formby Rd. ME8—1B 12
Formby Ter. ME2—1B 12
Forstal La. ME15—6B 24
Forstal Rd. ME20 & ME14—4A 20
Forsters. ME7—4J 29
Fort Pit Hill. ME14—7K 3
Fort Pit St. ME4—1K 7

Fort St. ME1—7J 3
Foster St. ME15—4J 23
Fostington Way. ME5—4E 14
Foulds Clo. ME8—7J 9
Fountain La. ME16—5C 22
Fountain Rd. ME2—2D 2
Fourth Av. ME7—7F 5
Fowey Clo. ME5—7D 8
Fowler Clo. ME8—2E 16
Foxburrow La. ME8—7A 10
Foxden Dri. ME15—6D 24
Foxglove Cres. ME5—1E 14
Fox St. ME5—5D 4
Francis Dri. ME5—3G 15
Francis La. ME15—3D 28
Franklin Clo. ME18—3B 24
Franklin Rd. ME7—6E 4
Franks Ct. ME8—2J 9
Frederick Rd. ME7—7D 4
Frederick St. ME4—1B 8
Freelands Rd. ME8—6D 12
Freeman Gdns. ME4—2A 8
Freeman Way. ME15—1C 28
Fremlins Rd. ME14—3G 25
Frensham Wlk. ME5—3F 15
Freshwater Rd. ME5—5C 8
Fresia Clo. ME7—6G 5
Friars Av. ME5—3F 15
Friary Pl. ME2—4G 3
Frindsbury Hill. ME2—2H 3
Frindsbury Rd. ME2—3G 3
Frinstead Clo. ME8—1K 9
Frinstead Wlk. ME16—7B 20
Frithwood Rd. ME15—6D 24
Frittenden Rd. ME2—1J 3
Frog La. ME19—6A 18
Froyle Clo. ME16—1E 22
Fui Ter. ME14—7G 21
Fulbert Dri. ME14—3E 24
Fullers Clo. ME14—3E 24
Fulmar Rd. ME2—7J 1
Fulme End. ME15—5F 23
Fuminger Cotts. ME15—3B 26
Furfield. ME15—3C 28
Furrell's Rd. ME1—6J 3

Gable Cotts. ME15—3J 27
(Loose)
Gable Cotts. ME15—1F 29
(Otham)
Gabriel's Hill. ME15—3J 23
Gads Hill. ME7—4G 5
Gainsborough Clo. ME8—6A 10
Galahad Av. ME2—5D 2
Galena Clo. ME5—4G 15
Gallants La. ME18—1B 26
Gandy's La. ME17—6A 28
Garden Clo. ME15—1C 28
Gardenia Clo. ME2—1G 3
Garden St. ME7—5B 4
Gardiner St. ME7—6D 4
Garfield Rd. ME7—5E 4
Garrington Clo. ME14—1A 24
Gas House Rd. ME1—5H 3
Gassons Rd. ME6—5C 12
Gatcombe Clo. ME5—7B 8
Gatland La. ME16—6C 22
Gault Clo. ME15—5E 24
Gayhurst Clo. ME8—6A 10
Geneva Av. ME8—2H 9
Gentian Clo. ME5—1E 14
Gentian Clo. ME14—2C 24
George Holding Centre. ME20
　　　　—2E 18
(off Chaucer Way.)
George La. ME1—6H 3
George Marsham Ho. ME17
　　　　—5H 27
George St. ME15—4J 23
Georgian Dri. ME17—5F 27
Georgian Way. ME8—1E 16
Gerald Av. ME4—2A 8
Gerrard Av. ME1—4J 7
Gibraltar Av. ME7—4B 4
Gibraltar Hill. ME4—7A 4
Gibralter La. ME14—6E 20
Gidds Pond Cotts. ME14—1C 24
Giddyhorn La. ME16—3E 22
Gigg Hill Rd. ME20—3D 18
Gilbert Clo. ME7—7H 9
Gilbert Ter. ME14—7G 21
Gill Av. ME2—1J 3
Gillingham Business Pk. ME7
　　　　—3H 9
Gillingham Grn. ME7—5F 5
Gillingham Rd. ME7—7D 4
Glade, The. ME5—3G 15
Gladstone Clo. ME7—2K 7
Gladstone Rd. ME14—1J 23
Gladwyn Clo. ME8—1F 17
Glamford Rd. ME2—6C 2
Glamis Clo. ME5—7B 8

Glanville Rd. ME2—4F 3
Glanville Rd. ME7—6E 4
Glasgow Ho. ME15—1C 28
(off Highland Rd.)
Gleaming Wood Dri. ME5—5J 15
Gleaners Clo. ME14—3C 24
Gleanings Mews. ME1—6H 3
Glebe La. ME16—6B 22
Glebe Rd. ME7—1F 9
Glebe, The. ME2—2B 6
Glencoe Rd. ME4—2B 8
Gleneagles Dri. ME15—6H 23
Glenwood Clo. ME5—3D 8
Glenwood Clo. ME7—6H 9
Glenwood Clo. ME16—2E 22
Glistening Glade. ME8—6B 10
Globe La. ME4—6A 4
(in two parts)
Gloucester Clo. ME8—4D 10
Gloucester Rd. ME15—7B 24
Glynne Clo. ME8—6A 10
Goad Av. ME5—2H 15
Godden Rd. ME6—5D 12
Goddings Dri. ME1—1F 7
Goddington Rd. ME2—3G 3
Godfrey Clo. ME2—2E 2
Golden Wood Clo. ME5—5K 15
Goldfinch Clo. ME20—4E 18
Golding Clo. ME2—5G 19
Goldings, The. ME8—4K 9
Goldstone Wlk. ME5—4G 15
Goldthorne Clo. ME14—3A 24
Goodall Clo. ME8—7B 10
Goodwin Dri. ME14—6H 21
Goose Clo. ME5—5B 8
Gordon Rd. ME2—4F 3
Gordon Rd. ME4—2B 8
Gordon Rd. ME7—4B 4
(Brompton)
Gordon Rd. ME7—6F 5
(Gillingham)
Gordon Ter. ME1—7H 3
Gore Ct. Rd. ME15—3D 28
Gorham Clo. ME6—6D 12
Gorham Dri. ME15—6E 24
Gorse Av. ME5—1E 14
Gorse Cres. ME20—6H 19
Gorse Rd. ME2—3E 2
Gorst St. ME7—6D 4
Goudhurst Clo. ME16—3G 23
Goudhurst Rd. ME8—1J 9
Gould Rd. ME5—2H 15
Goulston. ME15—2A 26
Grace Av. ME1—1F 23
Grafton Av. ME1—4K 7
Graham Clo. ME7—5B 4
Grainey Field. ME9—7H 11
Grain Rd. ME8—1D 16
Grampian Way. ME15—6E 24
Granada St. ME15—3J 23
Granary Clo. ME8—3C 10
Granary Clo. ME14—2C 24
Grange Clo. ME19—4A 18
Grange Cotts. ME15—2G 29
Grange Hill. ME5—1C 8
Grange Ho. ME5—5C 22
Grange La. ME14—4F & 5F 21
Grange Rd. ME2—4G 3
Grange Rd. ME7—5F 5
Grange, The. ME19—7E 18
Grange Way. ME1—1H 7
Grant Clo. ME7—3J 9
Granville Rd. ME7—6F 5
Granville Rd. ME14—1J 23
Grapple Rd. ME14—7F 21
Grasmere Gro. ME2—1H 3
Grasslands. ME17—1G 17
Grassmere. ME19—4D 18
Grassy Glade. ME7—6J 9
Gravelly Bottom Rd. ME17—5K 29
Gravel Wlk. ME1—6J 3
Graveney Rd. ME15—1D 28
Gravesend Rd. ME8 & ME2
—2A to 4E 2
Gt. Lines. ME7—6B 4
Gt. South Av. ME4—3B 8
Grebe Ct. ME20—5D 18
Grecian St. ME14—1J 23
Greenbank. ME5—4C 8
Greenbank Clo. ME7—7H 9
Green Clo. ME1—2J 7
Greenfield. ME20—7A 14
Greenfield Cotts. ME14—3J 21
Greenfield Rd. ME7—5F 5
Greenfields. ME15—7C 24
Greenfields Clo. ME3—1J 3
Greenfinches. ME6—6G 9
Green Hill. ME15—6F 25
Greenhill Cotts. ME15—7F 25
Greenhithe. ME15—4H 23
Green La. ME17—6K 27
Green La. Cotts. ME17—5J 29

Greensand Rd. ME15—5E 24
Green's Cotts. ME15—4C 26
Greenside. ME15—4K 23
Green St. ME7—6D 4
Green, The. ME9—1K 11
Green, The. ME14—3G 25
Green, The. ME15—1D 26
Green, The. ME19—6A 18
Greenvale Gdns. ME8—2J 9
Greenview Wlk. ME7—7H 5
Greenway. ME5—6J 7
Green Way. ME16—4D 22
Greenways. ME14—2D 24
Greenwich Clo. ME5—1H 15
Greenwich Clo. ME16—3F 23
Gregory Clo. ME8—1G 17
Gresham Rd. ME17—5F 27
Greystone Rd. ME15—5E 24
Groombridge Sq. ME15—2D 28
Grosvenor Av. ME4—1K 7
Grosvenor Rd. ME15—3D 28
Grosvenor Rd. ME7—3G 9
Grove Grn. La. ME14—2C 24
Grove Grn. Rd. ME14—2D 24
Grove Rd. ME2—3G 3
Grove Rd. ME4—2C 8
Grove Rd. ME7—5H 5
Grove Rd. ME15—2A 28
Groves, The. ME6—6D 12
Grove, The. ME14—4E 24
Grovewood Dri. ME14—2C 24
Guardian Ct. ME8—3K 9
Guildford Gdns. ME2—5B 2
Guildford Ho. ME15—1B 28
(off Cambridge Cres.)
Gullands. ME17—4J 29
Gundulph Ho. ME1—5H 3
Gundulph Rd. ME4—7K 3
Gundulph Sq. ME1—5H 3
Gun La. ME2—4F 3
Guston Rd. ME14—2A 24

Hacket Ho. ME14—7G 21
Hackney Rd. ME16—5E 22
Hadleigh Cl. ME7—2C 16
Hadlow Rd. ME14—2A 24
Haig Av. ME1—3J 7
Haig Av. ME2—8B 8
Haig Av. ME7—7F 5
Halden Clo. ME20—3D 28
Hale Rd. ME20—5J 19
Halifax Clo. ME5—6C 8
Halling By-Pass. ME2—1B & 1E 12
Hall Rd. ME5—2J 15
Hallsfield Rd. ME5—2D 14
Hallwood Clo. ME8—7A 10
Halstead Wlk. ME16—7C 20
Halstow Clo. ME15—2K 27
Hambledon Ct. ME16—4D 22
Hambrose Hill. ME5—2D 8
Hamelin Rd. ME7—3G 9
Hamilton Ho. ME15—3C 28
Hamilton Rd. ME7—4E 4
Ham La. ME3—2K 15
Hammond Hill. ME4—7K 3
Hampshire Clo. ME5—5D 8
Hampshire Dri. ME15—7A 24
Hampson Way. ME14—3E 24
Hampton Clo. ME5—7B 8
Hampton Rd. ME14—1A 24
Hamwick Grn. ME5—4J 15
Hanover Dri. ME8—1E 16
Hanover Grn. ME20—3C 18
Hanover Rd. ME17—5E 26
Hanway. ME8—2H 9
Harbourland Clo. ME14—6H 21
Harcourt Gdns. ME8—1G 17
Hardie Clo. ME19—5D 18
Hardinge Clo. ME8—1F 17
Hards Town. ME4—7B 4
Hardwick Rd. ME15—7C 24
Hardy St. ME14—1J 23
Harebell Clo. ME5—1E 14
Harebell Clo. ME14—2C 24
Haredale Clo. ME1—5J 7
Hare St. ME4—1C 8
Harold Av. ME7—7F 5
Harold Rd. ME1—1B 6
Harp Farm Rd. ME14—6J 15
Harptree Dri. ME5—7K 7
Harrow Cotts. ME17—4J 29
Harrow Rd. ME7—6G 9
Hartington St. ME4—1B 8
Hartley Clo. ME15—2D 28
Hartlip Hill. ME9—5H 11
Hartnup St. ME16—5E 22
Hartpiece Clo. ME8—2C 10
Hart St. ME16—4H 23
Harty Av. ME8—2D 16
Harvel Av. ME4—4E 2
Harvesters Clo. ME8—6B 10
Harvesters Way. ME14—3B 24

Harvest Ridge. ME19—4B 18
Harvey Rd. ME8—4B 10
Harwood Rd. ME8—3E 10
Haslemere Parkwood Est. ME15
—3D 28
Haste Hill Clo. ME17—5J 27
Haste Hill Rd. ME17—5J 27
Hastings Rd. ME15—4K 23
Hatfield Rd. ME2—3F 3
Hatherall Rd. ME14—1K 23
Hatton Rd. ME5—2J 15
Havant Wlk. ME15—2D 28
Haven Clo. ME1—2H 7
Havisham Clo. ME1—2J 7
Havock La. ME14—3H 23
Hawbeck Rd. ME8—3H 9
Hawkhurst Rd. ME8—1H 9
Hawkins Clo. ME4—5A 4
Hawkwood Clo. ME1—6J 3
Hawley Ct. ME16—3G 23
Hawser Rd. ME1—3H 7
Hawthorne Av. ME8—3K 9
Hawthorn Rd. ME2—5C 2
Hawthorn Rd. ME5—7A 8
Hawthorns. ME5—4F 15
Hawthorns, The. ME20—5J 19
Hayes Clo. ME2—3J 9
Hayfield. ME19—4C 18
Hayle Mill Cotts. ME15—7H 23
Hayle Mill Rd. ME15—6H 23
Hayle Rd. ME15—4J 23
Hayley Clo. ME2—2A 6
Haymen St. ME4—1K 7
Hayward's Ho. ME1—5H 3
Haywood Av. ME2—3G 3
Hazel Av. ME16—2E 22
Hazel Gro. ME5—4C 8
Hazels, The. ME8—7J 9
Hazlemere Dri. ME7—6G 5
Hazlitt Dri. ME16—2F 23
Headcorn Rd. ME8—7J 5
Headingley Rd. ME16—1D 22
Head Race, The. ME15—5F 23
Heaf Gdns. ME20—5K 19
Heather Clo. ME5—1F 15
Heather Dri. ME15—5K 23
Heathfield. ME17—4J 29
Heathfield Av. ME14—7J 21
Heathfield Clo. ME5—4C 8
Heathfield Clo. ME14—7H 21
Heathfield Rd. ME14—7H 21
Heath Gro. ME16—5C 22
Heathorn St. ME14—2K 23
Heath Rd. ME15 & ME17
—3A 26 to 6D 28
(East Farleigh)
Heath Rd. ME16—4B 22
Heath Rd. ME17—4J 29
(Langley Heath)
Heathside Av. ME17—4E 26
Hedges, The. ME14—7G 21
Hedley St. ME14—2J 23
(in two parts)
Hempstead Rd. ME7—2B 16
Hempstead Valley Dri. ME7
—6H 9 to 2C 16
Henbane Clo. ME14—2C 24
Henley Clo. ME5—6B 8
Henley Rd. ME8—4A 10
Henry St. ME4—1C 8
Henry St. ME8—3D 10
Hepplewhite M. ME5—4F 15
Herbert Rd. ME4—1B 8
Herbert Rd. ME8—4B 10
Hereford Clo. ME8—2A 10
Hereford Rd. ME15—1B 28
Heritage Rd. ME5—6B 8
Herman Ter. ME4—1B 8
Hermitage La. ME16—1B to 4C 22
Hermitage La. ME20—6K 19
Hermitage Rd. ME3—2B 2
Herne Rd. ME8—2K 9
Heronden Rd. ME15—4D 28
Heron Rd. ME20—5D 18
Heron Way. ME5—7B 8
Hero Wlk. ME1—5H 7
Herts Cres. ME15—5H 27
Hever Clo. ME15—2D 28
Hever Croft. ME2—6E 2
Hever Gdns. ME16—4G 23
Hever Ho. ME2—2J 11
(off Cypress Rd.)
Hextable Clo. ME16—7C 20
Hickory Dell. ME7—6H 9
Hide Rd. ME16—1F 23
Higgins La. ME4—6A 4
Higham Clo. ME15—2D 28
Higham Rd. ME3—1J 3
High Banks. ME15—3H 27
Highberry. ME19—4C 18
Highcroft Grn. ME15—4D 28
High Dewar Rd. ME8—4D 10

High Elms. ME8—2B 10
Highfield Clo. ME8—5A 10
Highfield Rd. ME8—5A 10
Highgrove Rd. ME5—7B 8
Highland Rd. ME15—1C 28
Highlands Clo. ME2—6C 2
High Ridge. ME7—3G 9
High St. Aylesford, ME20—3K 19
High St. Brompton, ME7—5B 4
High St. Chatham, ME4
—7K 3 & 7B 4
High St. East Malling, ME19—7E 18
High St. Gillingham, ME7—5D 4
(in three parts)
High St. Halling, ME2—2B 12
High St. Maidstone, ME14—3H 23
High St. Rainham, ME8—3B 10
High St. Rochester, ME1
—5H 3 to 7A 4
(in three parts)
High St. Snodland, ME6—5E 12
High St. Strood, ME2—4F 3
High St. Upper Upnor, ME2—2A 4
High St. West Malling, ME19
—6A 18
High St. Wouldham, ME1—1G 13
High View. ME3—1B 2
Highview Clo. ME15—7J 23
Highview Dri. ME5—7J 7
Highwoods Clo. ME3—1B 2
Hilborough Gro. ME5—2G 15
Hilda Rd. ME4—1B 8
Hildenborough Cres. ME16—7B 20
Hilden Shaw. ME15—7J 23
Hillary Rd. ME14—7G 21
Hill Chase. ME5—2E 14
Hill Crest. ME15—3J 27
Hillcrest Dri. ME2—2B 6
Hillcrest Rd. ME4—2A 8
Hill Grn. Rd. ME9—4K 17
Hill Rd. ME1—2F 7
(Wouldham)
Hill Rd. ME1—7D 6
(Wouldham)
Hillshaw Cres. ME2—6C 2
Hillside. ME1—2F 7
Hillside Av. ME2—3G 3
Hillside Cotts. ME16—5C 20
Hillside Rd. ME4—7B 4
Hill's Ter. ME4—1A 8
Hilltop. ME5—5A 26
Hilltop Rd. ME2—2H 3
Hill View Way. ME5—7K 7
Hillyfield Clo. ME2—2E 2
Hinton Cres. ME7—6H 9
Hirley Av. ME5—7J 7
Hoath Clo. ME8—5J 9
Hoath La. ME8—5J 9
Hoath Way. ME8—5J 9
Hockers La. ME14—1D 24
Hodgson Cres. ME6—4E 12
Holborn La. ME4—6A 4
Holborough Rd. ME6—5E 12
Holcombe Rd. ME1—1H 7
Holcombe Rd. ME4—2A 8
Holding St. ME8—3C 10
Holland Rd. ME5—1E 14
Holland Rd. ME14—2J 23
Hollingbourne Rd. ME8—1K 9
Hollingworth Rd. ME15—3D 28
Hollow La. ME6—6D 12
Hollow La. ME9—7H 11
Holly Clo. ME5—3D 8
Holly Clo. ME7—5F 5
Holly Farm Rd. ME15—2G 29
Holly Rd. ME2—5D 2
(Strood)
Holly Rd. ME2—1J 3
(Wainscott)
Hollytree Dri. ME3—2A 2
Holly Vs. ME14—3G 25
(off Street, The.)
Holly Vs. ME15—2A 26
Hollywood Ho. ME5—3J 15
Hollywood La. ME3—1G 3
Holmoaks. ME8—2B 10
Holmoaks. ME14—2A 24
Holmside. ME2—2F 9
Holt Wood Av. ME20—6H 19
Holtwood Clo. ME8—7A 10
Holtye Cres. ME15—5K 23
Holywell La. ME9—2J 11
Homesdale Clo. ME17—5H 27
Honduras Ter. ME14—7G 21
Hone St. ME2—3G 3
Honeybee Glade. ME8—6B 10
Honey Clo. ME7—7H 9
Honey La. ME15—2F 29
Honeypot Clo. ME7—7H 9
Honeysuckle Clo. ME5—1E 14
Hook Clo. ME5—7K 7
Hook Rd. ME6—5D 12
Hooper's Pl. ME1—7H 3

34

Hooper's Rd. ME1—7H 3
Hoo Rd. ME3—1J 3
Hope Cotts. ME15—3J 27
Hope St. ME4—1B 8
Hope St. ME14—1H 23
Hopewell Dri. ME5—4D 8
Hornbeam Av. ME5—3H 15
Hornbeam Clo. ME20—5F 19
Horseshoe Rd. ME7—7G 9
Horsewash La. ME1—5H 3
Horsham La. ME8 & ME9—1F 11
Horshoes La. ME17—4H 29
Horsley Rd. ME1—7G 3
Horsted Av. ME4—3K 7
Horsted Retail Pk. ME5—7J 7
Horsted Way. ME4—5J 7
Horton Downs. ME15—6D 24
Horwood Clo. ME1—4G 7
Hospital La. ME1—7K 3
Hothfield Rd. ME8—3C 10
Houghton Av. ME7—2D 16
House, The. ME14—4J 21
Howard Av. ME1—7J 3
Howard Dri. ME16—1D 22
Howard Ho. ME4—4F 23
Howard Rd. ME19—6D 18
Howbury Wlk. ME8—1F 17
Howick Rd. ME20—6K 19
Hubbard's La. ME17—6J 27
Hubble Dri. ME15—1C 28
Huckleberry Clo. ME5—2H 15
Hughes Dri. ME2—1J 3
Humber Cres. ME2—4E 2
Humber Ho. ME15—7C 24
Hunstanton Clo. ME8—2G 17
Hunters Way. ME7—3F 9
Hunters Way W. ME5—2E 8
Huntingdon Wlk. ME15—1C 28
Huntington Rd. ME17—5D 26
Hunton Hill. ME15—7B 26
Huntsman Clo. Ct. ME4—3J 7
Huntsmans Clo. ME4—3K 7
Huntsmans La. ME14
—3K 23 & 2A 24
(in two parts)
Hurst Clo. ME5—6K 7
Hurst Hill. ME5—3E 14
Hurstings, The. ME15—5F 23
Hurst Pl. ME4—4C 10
Hurst Way. ME5—5B 22
Hurstwood. ME5—1E 14
Hurstwood Rd. ME7 & ME14
—7D to 4D 16
Hutsford Clo. ME8—7A 10
Hyacinth Rd. ME2—5C 2
Hybrid Clo. ME1—3J 7
Hyperion Dri. ME2—2E 2

Iden Rd. ME2—2H 3
Idenwood Clo. ME8—7A 10
Illustrious Clo. ME5—7B 8
Imperial Rd. ME7—1D 8
Impton La. ME5—4G 15
Ingle Rd. ME4—2A 8
Ingram Rd. ME7—6F 5
Inner Lines. ME7—5B 4
Institute Rd. ME4—7B 4
Inverness Rd. ME15—1C 28
(off Lancashire Rd.)
Iona Clo. ME5—4K 15
Iona Rd. ME15—2J 27
Iris Clo. ME5—5G 15
Ironside Clo. ME5—4B 8
Irvine Rd. ME3—2A 2
Iversgate Clo. ME8—2C 10
Ivy Pl. ME1—2F 7
Ivy St. ME8—4C 10

Jacklin Clo. ME5—3F 15
Jackson Av. ME1—4K 7
Jamaica Ter. ME14—7G 21
James Rd. ME2—2A 6
James St. ME1—7H 3
James St. ME4—7A 4
James St. ME7—5D 4
James St. ME14—2J 23
Jarrett Av. ME2—1H 3
Jarvis Ho. ME14—7F 21
Jasmine Clo. ME5—1F 15
Jasmine Rd. ME19—6D 18
Jasmine Rd. ME19—6D 18
Jasper Av. ME1—2H 7
Jeffery St. ME7—5D 4
Jeffrey St. ME14—2J 23
Jeffries Cotts. ME15—5A 26
Jellicoe Pavilion. ME20—6K 19
Jenkins Dale. ME4—1A 8
Jenkins Dri. ME15—3C 28
Jenner Rd. ME1—7H 3
Jenner Way. ME20—7K 13
Jerome Rd. ME20—2D 18
Jersey Rd. ME2—4F 3

Jeyes Rd. ME7—7D 4
Jezreels Rd. ME7—1E 8
Jiniwin Rd. ME1—5J 7
Johannesburg Ho. ME15—3C 28
John St. ME1—7H 3
John St. ME14—1J 23
Joiners Ct. ME4—2C 8
Jordan Clo. ME15—3C 28
Jubilee Ter. ME7—5D 4
Junction Rd. ME7—7E 4
Juniper Clo. ME5—1G 15

Keats Rd. ME20—3D 18
Keepers Cotts. ME14—1G 25
Kellaway Rd. ME5—3G 15
Kemp Clo. ME5—1E 14
Kempton Clo. ME5—2J 15
Kemsley St. Rd. ME7—3D 16
Kendal Pl. ME15—7A 24
Kendal Way. ME8—4A 10
Kenilworth Dri. ME8—5A 10
Kenilworth Gdns. ME5—5A 10
Kenilworth Ho. ME16—5D 22
Kennard Clo. ME1—2E 6
Kennington Clo. ME8—7K 5
Kennington Clo. ME15—1D 28
Kensington Ho. ME16—5C 22
Kent Av. ME15—6B 24
Kent Clo. ME1—4H 7
Kent Ho. ME15—4J 23
Kent Rd. ME2—1B 12
Kent Rd. ME6—7E 12
Kenward Rd. ME16—2E 22
Kenwood Av. ME5—1G 15
Kenya Ter. ME14—7G 21
Kenyon Wlk. ME8—2D 16
Kestrel Rd. ME5—3J 15
Kettle La. ME15—3A 26
Kewlands. ME14—1A 24
Keyes Av. ME4—2A 8
Khartoum Rd. ME4 & ME7—6A 4
Khyber Rd. ME4 & ME7—4C 4
Kilburn Ho. ME14—2J 23
Kiln Barn Rd. ME20—6G 19
Kilndown Clo. ME16—7C 20
Kimberley Rd. ME7—1E 8
King Arthurs Dri. ME2—2E 2
King Edward Rd. ME1—6H 3
King Edward Rd. ME4—2A 8
King Edward Rd. ME7—5G 5
King Edward Rd. ME15—5H 23
Kingfisher Dri. ME5—5D 8
Kingfisher Rd. ME20—4D 18
King George Rd. ME5—2E 14
Kings Acre. ME15—6E 24
King's Av. ME1—1H 7
Kings Bastion. ME7—6B 4
Kingsdale Ct. ME15—3D 8
Kingsdown Clo. ME7—1C 16
Kingsdown Clo. ME16—3G 23
Kingsgate Clo. ME16—3E 22
Kingsley Rd. ME15—4J 23
Kings Orchard. ME1—6H 3
Kings Rd. ME5—3E 8
Kingston Cres. ME15—1H 15
Kingston Dri. ME15—7J 23
King St. ME1—6H 3
King St. ME4—7B 4
King St. ME7—6D 4
King St. ME14—3J 23
King St. ME19—6A 18
Kingsway. ME5 & ME7—3F 9
Kingswood Av. ME5—2K 7
Kingswood Rd. ME7—5E 4
Kingswood Rd. ME20—5D 14
Kingsworth Rd. ME8—7K 5
King William Rd. ME7—4D 4
Kinross Clo. ME5—5C 8
Kipling Dri. ME5—3D 18
Kirkdale. ME15—3H 27
Kirkdale Clo. ME5—3K 15
Kirkdale Cotts. ME15—3H 27
Kirkdale Rd. ME15—2H 27
Kitchener Av. ME4—3A 8
Kitchener Rd. ME2—3F 3
Kit Hill Av. ME5—2E 14
Knaves Acre Ct. ME8—7A 10
Knight Av. ME7—5E 4
Knightrider St. ME15—4J 23
Knight Rd. ME2—6F 3
Knole Rd. ME5—2J 15
Knowle Rd. ME1—1G 13
Knowle Rd. ME14—1J 23
Kyetop Wlk. ME8—6A 10

Laburnum Dri. ME20—4E 18
Laburnum Rd. ME2—6D 2
Lacey Clo. ME17—4J 29
Ladbrooke Ho. ME14—2J 23
Ladywood Rd. ME2—2A 6
Lakelands. ME15—1J 27
Laker Rd. ME1 & ME5—6H 7

Lakeside. ME6—7D 12
Lakeview Clo. ME6—7E 12
Lakewood Dri. ME8—6K 9
Lambard Ho. ME14—2J 23
Lamberhurst Grn. ME8—1J 9
Lamberhurst Rd. ME16—7B 20
Lambes Ct. ME8—7A 10
Lambeth Clo. ME1—5J 7
Lambourne Pl. ME8—2D 10
Lambourne Rd. ME15—5D 24
Lambourn Way. ME5—2J 15
Lambsfrith Gro. ME7—2D 16
Lamplighters Clo. ME7—7G 9
Lancashire Rd. ME15—1C 28
Lancaster Ct. ME8—5K 9
Lancelot Av. ME2—5D 2
Lancelot Clo. ME2—5D 2
Lancet La. ME15—2H 27
Landor Ct. ME7—2C 16
Landrail Rd. ME9—1K 11
Land Way. ME3—1C 2
Landway, The. ME14—4D 24
Langdale Clo. ME8—3K 9
Langdale Rise. ME16—2E 22
Langdon Rd. ME1—7H 3
Langham Gro. ME16—3E 22
Langley Pk. Farm Cotts. ME17
—4F 29
Langton Clo. ME14—2A 24
Lankester Parker Rd. ME1—6H 7
Lansdowne Av. ME15—2A 28
Lansdowne Ct. ME4—7A 4
Lansdowne Rd. ME4—2K 7
La Providence. ME1—6H 3
Larch Clo. ME20—4F 19
Larchcroft. ME5—1G 15
Larches, The. ME3—2B 2
Larch Wood Clo. ME5—4K 15
Larkfield Av. ME7—7F 5
Larkfield Clo. ME20—5E 18
Larkfield Rd. ME20—5E 18
Larkfield Trading Est. ME20
—1F 19
Larkin Clo. ME2—1G 3
Larkspur Clo. ME19—5E 18
Larkspur Rd. ME5—1E 14
Larkspur Rd. ME19—5D 18
Launder Way. ME15—5G 23
Laura Pl. ME1—2E 6
Laurel Ct. ME2—4E 2
Laurel Rd. ME7—4D 4
Laurel Wlk. ME8—6B 10
Lavenda Clo. ME7—1C 16
Lavender Clo. ME5—1G 15
Lavender Rd. ME19—6D 18
Lavender Rd. ME19—6D 18
Lavenders Rd. ME19—7A 18
Lavender Wlk. ME19—6D 18
Lawn Clo. ME2—2C 8
Lawrence Clo. ME15—1J 27
Lawrence St. ME7—6D 4
Laxton Clo. ME15—4D 24
Laxton Dri. ME17—7E 28
Layfield Rd. ME7—4G 5
Leafy Glade. ME8—6J 9
Leake Ho. ME1—3H 7
Leander Rd. ME1—5H 7
Leander Wlk. ME1—5H 7
Leeds Ho. ME2—2H 3
(off Cypress Rd.)
Leeds Rd. ME17—6H 29
Leeds Sq. ME8—1J 9
Lee Rd. ME5—3C 8
Lee Rd. ME6—4D 12
Leeward Rd. ME1—3H 7
Left Clo. ME7—5F 5
Legge La. ME6—6B 12
Leicester Rd. ME15—1B 28
Leigh Av. ME15—2K 27
Lendrim Clo. ME7—5B 4
(off Westcourt St.)
Leney Cotts. ME2—2A 12
Lenfield Av. ME14—3K 23
Lenham Way. ME8—1H 9
Lenside Dri. ME15—5E 24
Leonard Clo. ME16—1D 22
Leonard Rd. ME4—1C 8
Leopold Rd. ME4—1B 8
Lesley Pl. ME16—2G 23
Leslie Rd. ME7—4E 4
Lestead La. ME17—6F 29
Lester Rd. ME1—1B 8
Letchworth Av. ME4—3A 8
Lewis Av. ME8—2J 9
Lewis Ct. ME8—2J 9
Lewis Rd. ME17—5K 27
Leybourne Clo. ME5—3G 15
Leybourne Rd. ME2—3E 2
Leybourne Way. ME20—2C 18
Leyton Av. ME7—3F 9
Libya Ter. ME14—7G 21
Lichfield Clo. ME8—2A 10
Lichfield Ho. ME15—1C 28

Lidsing Rd. ME7 & ME14
—3B to 6A 16
Lidsing Rd. ME14—2H 21
Lilac Cres. ME2—5D 2
Lilac Grn. ME19—5E 18
Lilac Rd. ME2—6D 2
Lilk Hill. ME15—4F 25
Lilleburn. ME18—4B 18
Lime Ct. ME8—2E 16
Lime Cres. ME19—7E 18
Limetree Clo. ME5—4C 8
Linacre Clo. ME8—6A 10
Lincoln Clo. ME2—5C 2
Lincoln Rd. ME7—4E 4
Lincoln Rd. ME15—7A 24
Linden Ho. ME5—1F 15
Linden Rd. ME7—6F 5
Linden Rd. ME15—4D 26
Lindens, The. ME20—4J 19
Lines Ter. ME4—7B 4
Lingley Dri. ME3—1H 3
Links, The. ME5—4C 8
Linkway. ME20—5G 19
Linton Gore. ME17—5F 27
Linton Hill. ME17—7G 27
Linton Rd. ME15—6H 27
Linwood Av. ME2—3D 2
Lismore Clo. ME15—1J 27
Lister Clo. ME19—6D 18
Listmas Rd. ME4—1C 8
Littlebourne Av. ME8—7J 5
Littlebourne Rd. ME14—1A 24
Lit. Buckland Av. ME16—1F 23
Little St. ME16—5F 23
Little John Av. ME5—3F 15
Lit. Market Row. ME19—4C 18
Lit. Orchard. ME17—6F 29
Lit. Oxley. ME19—4C 18
Liverpool Ho. ME15—1B 28
(off Middlesex Rd.)
Livingstone Cir. ME7—6E 4
Livingstone Rd. ME7—6F 5
Livingstone Wlk. ME15—3D 28
Llandaff Ho. ME15—1B 28
(off Middlesex Av.)
Lobella Clo. ME7—5F 5
Locharno Av. ME8—2H 9
Lock Cotts. ME16—5D 20
Lockington Gro. ME1—6H 3
Lock La. ME14—5D 20
Locksley Clo. ME5—3E 14
Lock St. ME7—6C 4
Loddington La. ME17—7J 27
Lombarde Clo. ME2—1E 12
Lombardy Clo. ME7—6H 9
Lombardy Dri. ME14—3A 24
Londonderry Ho. ME15—1C 28
London Rd. ME2—4F 3
London Rd. ME8—3J 9
London Rd. ME9—4F 11
London Rd. ME16—7B 20 to 3G 23
London Rd. ME19—5A 18
London Rd. ME20—5H to 6K 19
(Ditton)
London Rd. ME20—5D 18
(Larkfield)
London Rd. E. ME20—6K 19
Long Catlis Rd. ME8—2F 17
Longfellow Rd. ME7—1D 8
Longfield Pl. ME15—7A 24
Longford Clo. ME8—4D 10
Longhamcopse. ME15—6D 24
Longhill Av. ME5—7C 4
Longhurst Dri. ME5—3F 15
Longley Rd. ME1—7H 3
Longley Rd. ME8—3C 10
Longparish Clo. ME15—2D 28
Long Rede La. ME16—4B 22
Longshaw Rd. ME15—3D 28
Longsole Cotts. ME16—4B 22
Lonsdale Dri. ME8—6A 10
Loose Ct. ME15—1J 27
Loose Hill. ME15—1J 27
Loose Rd. ME15—3J 27 to 5J 23
Lords Wood Clo. ME5—3A 15
Lords Wood La. ME5—3H 15
Lordswood Ind. Est. ME5—5K 15
Lords Wood La. ME5—3H 15
Louisville Av. ME7—7E 4
Lovelace Clo. ME8—7A 10
Love La. ME1—6H 3
Lwr. Bell La. ME20—4F 19
Lwr. Boxley Rd. ME14—2H 23
Lwr. East Rd. ME4—3C 4
Lwr. Fant Rd. ME16—5F 23
Lwr. Hartlip Rd. ME9—7H 11
Lwr. Rainham Rd. ME7 & ME8
—5H 5 to 2E 10
Lower Rd. ME15—1A 26 to 7F 23
(East Farleigh)
Lower Rd. ME15—4K 23
(Maidstone)
Lwr. Rochester Rd. ME3—1F 3

Lwr. Stone St. ME15—3J 23
Lwr. Tovil. ME15—5G 23
Lwr. Twydall Lane. ME8—7J 5
Lwr. Warren Rd. ME20—7E 14
Lwr. Woodlands Rd. ME7—5G 5
Lubbock Clo. ME15—3C 28
Lubbock Wlk. ME8—7A 10
Lucas Rd. ME6—6C 12
Lucerne St. ME14—2J 23
Luck's Hill. ME19—6A 18
Ludenham Clo. ME14—1A 24
Lughorse La. ME15—7A 26
Lullingstone Rd. ME16—7C 20
Lumsden Ter. ME4—7K 3
Lunsford La. ME20—1D to 5D 18
Lushington Rd. ME14—7E 20
Luton High St. ME5—2D 8
Luton Rd. ME4—7C 8
Lyall Way. ME8—1G 17
Lydd Rd. ME5—7C 8
Lyle Clo. ME2—2G 3
Lyminge Clo. ME8—2K 9
Lymington Ct. ME15—4D 28
Lyndhurst Av. ME8—5K 9
Lyndhurst Rd. ME15—7A 24
Lynette Av. ME2—2F 3
Lynors Av. ME2—2F 3
Lynstead Ho. ME16—6C 22
Lynstead Rd. ME8—1J 9
Lynton Dri. ME5—2H 15

McAlpine Cres. ME15—5H 27
Macauley Clo. ME20—2E 18
McCudden Row. ME7—5B 4
(off Middle St.)
MacDonald Rd. ME7—5E 4
Mackenders Clo. ME20—7A 14
Mackenders La. ME20—7A 14
McKenzie Clo. ME20—6K 19
McKenzie Rd. ME5—2G 15
Macklands Way. ME8—2D 10
McPhie Ho. ME14—7F 21
Madden Av. ME5—7K 7
Madginford Clo. ME15—5E 24
Madginford Rd. ME15—5D 24
Madras Ho. ME15—3C 28
(off Bell Rd.)
Mafeking Rd. ME5—2F 15
Magdalen Clo. ME7—1C 16
Magnolia Av. ME8—7J 9
Magpie Clo. ME20—5E 18
Magpie Hall Rd. ME4—4A 8
Magpie La. ME4—4G 17
Maida Rd. ME4—2C 8
Maidstone Rd. ME1—2H 7
Maidstone Rd. ME4—5K 7
Maidstone Rd. ME5—4D 14
Maidstone Rd. ME5—4D 14
(Blue Bell Hill)
Maidstone Rd. ME7—3D 16
Maidstone Rd. ME8—2E 16 to 6K 9
Maidstone Rd. ME17—5H 29
Mailyns, The. ME8—5A 10
Main Ga. Rd. ME4—4A & 3B 4
Malden Dri. ME14—6F 21
Mallard Wlk. ME20—4D 18
Mallard Way. ME15—6E 24
Malling Rd. ME19—1C 18 to 5E 12
Mallings Dri. ME14—3G 25
Mallings La. ME14—3G 25
Malling Ter. ME16—3E 22
Mallow Way. ME15—1F 15
Malta Av. ME5—5B 8
Malta Ter. ME14—7G 21
Malthouse Hill. ME15—4H 27
Maltings, The. ME8—4D 10
Maltings, The. ME14—2C 24
Malvern Rd. ME7—2F 9
Mamignot Clo. ME14—2E 24
Manchester Clo. ME5—6D 8
Mandeville Ct. ME14—2J 23
Mangravet Av. ME15—1A 28
Manningham Ho. ME19—7E 18
Manor Clo. ME14—4F 25
Manor Cotts. ME14—3G 29
Manor Ho. Cotts. ME14—3G 25
(off Green, The.)
Manor Ho. Dri. ME14—4F 23
Manor La. ME1—1E 6
Manor Rise. ME14—3F 25
Manor Rd. ME4—7A 4
Manor St. ME7—5B 4
Mansel Dri. ME1—2F 7
Mansfield Wlk. ME16—5G 23
Mansion Row. ME7—5B 4
Maple Av. ME7—6F 5
Maple Av. ME16—1E 22
Maple Clo. ME20—4E 18
Maple Rd. ME7—5E 4
Maplesden Clo. ME16—4B 22
Maplins Clo. ME8—3C 10
Marathon Paddock. ME7—7E 4

Mardale Clo. ME8—3D 10
Marden Rd. ME2—2H 3
Margate Clo. ME7—5F 5
Margetts Pl. ME2—1B 4
Marion Clo. ME5—3G 15
Marion Cres. ME15—6K 23
Market Bldgs. ME14—3H 23
Market Pl. ME4—7B 4
Market St. ME14—3H 23
Markham Cotts. ME15—2A 26
Marlborough Pde. ME16—5B 22
(off Beverley Rd.)
Marlborough Rd. ME7—7C 4
Marley Way. ME1—2H 7
Marlow Copse. ME5—4F 15
Marlowe Rd. ME20—3D 18
Marshall Rd. ME8—5K 9
Marsham Cres. ME17—7F 29
Marsham St. ME14—3J 23
Marsh Rd. ME2—2B 12
Marsh St. ME2—4G 3
Marsh Way. ME20—2E 18
Marstan Clo. ME9—2H 11
Marston Clo. ME5—2K 1
Marston Dri. ME14—2K 23
Marston Wlk. ME5—2E 14
Martin Rd. ME2—3G 3
Martin Sq. ME20—4E 18
Mary Dukes Pl. ME15—4K 23
Maryland Ct. ME8—7B 10
Maryland Rd. ME16—5B 22
Masefield Way. ME20—2D 18
Masters La. ME14—1A 18
Matfield Cres. ME14—2A 24
Matilda Clo. ME8—3J 9
Matts Hill Rd. ME9—3F 17
Maunders Clo. ME5—4D 8
Maxwell Dri. ME16—1D 22
Maxwell Rd. ME7—6B 4
Mayfair. ME2—3H 3
Mayfair Av. ME15—7J 23
Mayfield Clo. ME8—2B 10
Mayfield Cotts. ME14—3G 25
Mayford Rd. ME5—3K 15
Maynard Pl. ME2—2E 8
May Rd. ME1—1H 7
May Rd. ME7—7F 3
May's Cotts. ME15—4C 26
(East Farleigh)
May's Cotts. ME15—7A 22
(Kettle Corner)
May St. ME2—2A 6
May St. ME6—5F 13
May Ter. ME7—4B 4
Maywood Av. ME5—1E 14
Mead Grn. ME5—2J 15
Meadowbank Rd. ME4—7C 4
Meadow Clo. ME2—1C 12
Meadow Clo. ME5—7A 8
Meadow Cres. ME2—1C 12
Meadowdown Clo. ME7—1C 16
Meadow View Rd. ME17—5K 27
Meadow Wlk. ME6—6D 12
Meadow Wlk. ME14—4K 23
Meadside Wlk. ME5—6A 8
Mead, The. ME19—4C 18
Medina Rd. ME20—5G 19
Medlar Gro. ME7—1C 16
Medlars, The. ME14—1B 24
Medway Homes. ME4—3K 7
Medway Ho. ME15—7B 24
Medway Rd. ME7—4D 4
(in two parts)
Medway St. ME4—6A 4
Medway St. ME14—3H 23
Medway View. ME1—7J 3
Medway Vs. ME15—1D 26
Meeting Ho. La. ME4—7A 4
Megby Clo. ME8—6A 10
Melbourne Rd. ME4—1B 8
Melody Clo. ME8—1E 16
Melrose Clo. ME15—1J 27
Melville Ct. ME4—5A 4
Melville Rd. ME15—4J 23
Mercer Way. ME17—7F 29
Mercury Clo. ME1—1F 7
Meresborough Rd. ME8—2H 17
Mereworth Clo. ME8—1H 9
Mereworth Ho. ME2—2H 3
(off Cypress Rd.)
Meridian Ct. ME16—3G 23
Merivale Gro. ME5—1H 15
Merlin Av. ME20—4D 18
Merlin Rd. ME2—2F 3
Merrals Wood Rd. ME2—6C 2
Merriams Farm Cotts. ME17
—7H 25
Merton Clo. ME5—1J 15
Merton Rd. ME15—5D 24
Mews, The. ME2—4E 2
Mews, The. ME16—2G 23
Micawber Clo. ME5—4G 15

Middlefields. ME8—4D 10
Middle Row. ME14—3H 23
Middlesex Rd. ME15—1B 28
Middle St. ME7—5B 4
Middleton Clo. ME8—1G 17
Midhurst Clo. ME15—4J 23
Midley Clo. ME16—7C 20
Midsummer Rd. ME6—5C 12
Mierscourt Clo. ME8—4D 10
Mierscourt Rd. ME8—1G 17
Milburn Rd. ME7—4D 4
Miles Pl. ME1—1J 7
Milford Clo. ME16—2E 22
Military Rd. ME4—7A 4
Millbrook. ME19—5B 18
Mill Clo. ME2—2G 3
Millers Wharf. ME15—5F 23
Miller Way. ME2—1H 3
Millfordhope Rd. ME2—4B 2
Millhall. ME20—4H 19
Mill Hall Business Est. ME20
—4H 19
Mill Hall Rd. ME20—4H 19
Mill La. ME5—3D 8
Mill La. ME6—5F 13
Mill La. ME9—6H 11
Mill La. ME14—1H 23
Mill La. ME17—5F 27
Mill La. ME20—5D 18
Mill La. ME2—2G 3
Mill Rd. ME7—5D 4
Mills Ter. ME14—1B 8
Millstock Ter. ME15—5G 23
Mill St. ME6—5F 13
Mill St. ME15—3H 27
(Loose)
Mill St. ME15—3H 23
(Maidstone)
Mill St. ME19—7D 18
Milner Rd. ME7—4E 4
Milstead Clo. ME14—2A 24
Milstead Rd. ME8—2K 9
Milton Rd. ME7—7D 4
Milton St. ME15—6J 23
Mincers Clo. ME5—3J 15
Minerva St. ME2—3F 3
Minor Cannon Row. ME1—6H 3
Minster Rd. ME8—1K 9
Mitchell Av. ME4—2A 8
Mitre Rd. ME1—7G 3
Monarch Clo. ME5—6B 8
Monarch Hill. ME2—1C 12
Moncktons Av. ME14—7E 20
Moncktons Dri. ME14—7E 20
Moncktons La. ME14—7E 20
Monkdown. ME15—6E 24
Monkwood Clo. ME1—4G 7
Monmouth Clo. ME8—2A 10
Montfort Rd. ME2—3F 3
Montfort Rd. ME5—3F 15
Montgomery Av. ME5—5B 8
Montgomery Cotts. ME2—1C 12
Montgomery Rd. ME7—7D 4
Montrose Av. ME2—2F 9
Moore St. ME2—3F 3
Mooring Rd. ME1—3J 7
Moor Pk. Clo. ME8—4D 10
Moor St. ME8—4E 10
Morden Ct. ME1—7H 3
Morden St. ME1—7H 3
Morhen Clo. ME6—6C 12
Morris Rd. ME19—5D 18
Mossbank. ME5—2G 15
Mossy Glade. ME8—6B 10
Mostyn Rd. ME14—3A 24
Mote Av. ME15—4K 23
Mote Hall Vs. ME14—3G 25
Mote Rd. ME15—4J 23
Motney Hill Rd. ME8—1D 10
Motorway, M2. ME2, ME1, ME14,
ME7 & ME8—4A 2 to 1K 17
Motorway, M20. ME19, ME20 &
ME14—2A 18 to 4K 25
Mountbatten Av. ME3—1B 2
Mountbatten Av. ME5—5B 8
Mount Cotts. ME14—3F 25
Mount Dri. ME14—3F 25
Mount La. ME14—3F 25
Mt. Pleasant. ME5—7C 4
Mt. Pleasant. ME20—3A 20
Mount Rd. ME4—3C 4
Mount Rd. ME7—4B 4
Mount Rd. ME4—1A 8
Mountsfield Clo. ME16—2F 23
Mount, The. ME4—7A 4
Moyle Clo. ME8—1F 17
Muir Rd. ME15—4J 23
Mulberry Rd. ME7—1C 16
Mulberry Ct. ME14—2K 23
Munn's La. ME9—6H 11
Murray Rd. ME2—2H 3
Museum Av. ME14—2H 23
(off Week St.)

Museum St. ME14—3H 23
Mynn Cres. ME14—3E 24
Myrtle Cres. ME5—7A 8

Nagpur Ho. ME15—3C 28
Nag's Head La. ME1—7J 3
Napier Ct. ME14—7F 21
Napier Rd. ME7—1E 8
Napwood Clo. ME8—6A 10
Nares Rd. ME8—1F 17
Nash Clo. ME5—3J 15
Nashenden La. ME1—2E 6
Natal Rd. ME4—1B 8
Naylor's Cotts. ME7—4D 16
Neale St. ME4—2A 8
Nelson Ct. ME5—3D 8
Nelson Rd. ME5—3D 8
Nelson Ho. ME15—3D 28
Nelson Rd. ME1—1G 13
Nelson Rd. ME7—7E 4
Nelson Ter. ME5—3D 8
Neptune Clo. ME2—4K 3
Netley Clo. ME14—1B 24
Neville Clo. ME14—6H 21
Neville Rd. ME4—2C 8
Nevill Pl. ME6—6E 12
Nevill Pl. ME6—6E 12
Newark Ct. ME2—4G 3
Newark Yd. ME2—4G 3
New Barns Rd. ME14—6G 21
Newbury Av. ME16—7C 20
Newchurch Rd. ME15—6J 23
New Cotts. ME15—6A 26
New Covenant Pl. ME1—7J 3
New Cut. ME4—7A 4
New Cut. ME15—1F 27
New Cut Rd. ME14—3B 24
New Delhi Ho. ME15—3C 28
Newenden Clo. ME14—1B 24
Newenden Rd. ME1—7J 3
Newham St. ME4—1C 8
New Hythe Ho. ME20—2F 19
New Hythe La. ME20
—5E 18 to 2G 19
Newington Wlk. ME14—1A 24
Newnham Clo. ME8—7J 9
Newnham Ct. Cotts. ME14—7K 21
New Rd. ME1—4K 13
(Burham)
New Rd. ME1 & ME4—7J 3 & 7A 4
(Rochester)
New Rd. ME17—2G 29
New Rd. ME20 & ME19—6E 18
New Rd. ME20—5G 19
(Ditton)
New Rd. Av. ME4—7K 3
New Stairs. ME4—5A 4
New St. ME4—1K 7
Newton Clo. ME5—3J 15
Newton Clo. ME16—4G 23
Nicklaus Dri. ME5—2F 15
Nickleby Clo. ME1—2H 7
Nightingale Clo. ME8—6B 10
Nightingale Clo. ME20—4D 18
Nile Rd. ME7—7D 4
Nine Acres Rd. ME2—1A 6
Norah La. ME3—1A 2
Nore Clo. ME7—3F 9
Norfolk Clo. ME5—2J 15
Norfolk Clo. ME8—2A 10
Norfolk Rd. ME15—7A 24
Norman Clo. ME2—7E 2
Norman Clo. ME8—1D 16
Norman Clo. ME14—1K 23
Norman Rd. ME6—7E 12
Norman Rd. ME8—6A 18
Norreys Rd. ME8—5B 10
Norrington Rd. ME15—2J 27
North Bank Clo. ME2—6E 2
Northbourne Rd. ME8—7J 5
Northcote Rd. ME2—4F 3
North Cres. ME17—4F 27
N. Dane Way. ME5—3E 8 to 4A 16
Northdown Clo. ME14—7H 21
North Downs Ho. ME2—1C 12
Northfields. ME16—5B 22
Northfleet Clo. ME14—2A 24
N. Folly Rd. ME15—5A 26
N. Gate. ME1—5H 3
Northleigh Clo. ME15—2J 27
North Pole Rd. ME16—4A 22
North Rd. ME4—3C 4
North Rd. ME7—4B 4
North St. ME2—4G 3
North St. ME16—4A 22
North St. ME17—7J 29
Northumberland Av. ME8—3C 10
Northumberland Ct. ME15—1B 28
(off Northumberland Rd.)
Northumberland Rd. ME15—1A 28
North View. ME15—6K 23
North Way. ME14—7H 21
Norton Gro. ME5—1E 14

Norton Rd. ME17—7G 29
Norway Ter. ME14—7G 21
Norwich Clo. ME2—5C 2
Norwich Ho. ME15—1B 28
  (off Leicester Rd.)
Nottingham Av. ME15—1B 28
Nottingham Wlk. ME2—5C 2
Nursery Av. ME14—4F 25
Nursery Av. ME16—1D 22
Nursery Pk. Ind. Est. ME7, 7—5E 4
  (off Railway St.)
Nursery Rd. ME8—4A 10
Nursery Rd. ME20—5G 19
Nutfield Clo. ME5—4C 8

Oakapple La. ME16—4B 22
Oak Av. ME7—5F 5
Oak Av. ME14—3G 25
  (off Green, The.)
Oak Cotts. ME17—5K 27
Oak Dri. ME3—2A 2
Oak Dri. ME20—4E 18
Oakhurst Clo. ME5—2F 15
Oakland Clo. ME7—2F 15
Oak La. ME9—4F 11
Oakleigh Clo. ME5—3E 14
Oak Rd. ME2—5D 2
Oaks Dene. ME5—4F 15
Oaks, The. ME20—5J 19
Oak Ter. ME5—3G 15
Oak Tree Av. ME5—1A 28
Oakum Ct. ME4—2C 8
Oakwood Ct. ME16—4F 23
Oakwood Rd. ME16—4E 22
Oastview. ME4—4D 10
Odiham Dri. ME16—7C 20
Offham Rd. ME6A 18
Officers' Rd. ME4—4C 4
Old Barn Clo. ME7—6G 9
Old Barn Rd. ME19—4B 18
Old Carriage Way, The. ME7—1B 16
Old Castle Wlk. ME8—1F 17
Old Chatham Rd. ME14
—1E & 5E 20
(in two parts)
Old Dri. ME15—2H 27
Olde Manor Cotts. ME14—3G 25
  (off Green, The.)
Oldfield Clo. ME8—4A 10
Oldfield Clo. ME15—6C 24
Old House Rd. ME9—7H 11
Old Loose Clo. ME15—4H 27
Old Loose Hill. ME15—4H 27
Old Mill La. ME20—3C 20
Old Mill Rd. ME17—7K 25
Old Orchard La. ME19—5B 18
Old Pattens La. ME1—1J 7
Old Rd. ME4—7A 4
Old Salts La. ME15—4H 27
Old Tovil Rd. ME15—5H 23
Old Trafford Clo. ME16—1D 22
Old Tree La. ME17—5A 28
Old Watling St. ME2—3A 2
Old Well Ct. ME15—5G 23
Oliver Clo. ME4—2C 8
Oliver North Ho. ME15—1A 26
Olivers Cotts. ME14—3G 25
Olivine Clo. ME5—5G 15
Olliffes Clo. ME5—3F 15
Onslow Rd. ME1—1J 7
Opal Grn. ME5—3H 15
Orache Dri. ME4—2C 24
Orange Ter. ME1—6J 3
Orbit Clo. ME5—5G 15
Orchard Av. ME2—2E 2
Orchard Av. ME20—5J 19
Orchard Bank. ME17—7F 29
  (off Amber La.)
Orchard Clo. ME17—5E 26
  (Coxheath)
Orchard Clo. ME17—4J 29
  (Langley Heath)
Orchard Cotts. ME16—7C 22
Orchard Cotts. ME17—7E 28
  (off Amber La.)
Orchard Dri. ME9—7K 11
Orchard Dri. ME14—4C 24
Orchard Gro. ME20—4F 19
Orchard Pl. ME16—4G 23
Orchard St. ME8—5B 10
Orchard St. ME15—4J 23
Orchard Way. ME6—6D 12
Orchid Clo. ME5—5B 2
Ordnance St. ME4—1K 7
Ordnance Ter. ME4—7K 3
Oriel Ho. ME1—6H 3
Oriole Way. ME20—4D 18
Orion Rd. ME1—5H 7
Ormsby Grn. ME8—2G 17
Orwell Clo. ME20—3D 18
Orwell Ho. ME15—7C 24
Osborne Rd. ME7—6E 4

Osprey Av. ME5 & ME7—2F 9
Osprey Wlk. ME20—5D 18
Ostlers Ct. ME6—5E 12
Otham La. ME15—5G 25
Otham St. ME15—1F 29
Otterbourne Pl. ME15—6C 24
Otterham Quay. ME8—4E 10
Otteridge Rd. ME14—4E 24
Otway St. ME4—1B 8
Otway St. ME7—5E 4
Otway Ter. ME4—1B 8
Owen Clo. ME19—6D 18
Owens Way. ME7—5H 5
Oxford Rd. ME7—1E 8
Oxford Rd. ME15—7B 24
Oxford St. ME6—5E 12
Oxley Shaw La. ME19—5B 18

Paddlesworth Rd. ME6—4A 12
Paddock, The. ME4—7A 4
Pad's Hill. ME14—3J 23
Padsole La. ME15—3J 23
Paget St. ME7—6C 4
Pagitt St. ME4—2K 7
Palace Av. ME15—3J 23
Palace Ct. ME8—2E 8
Palm Cotts. ME15—4G 27
Palmerston Rd. ME4—4A 8
Panton Clo. ME5—1J 15
Papion Gro. ME5—3E 14
Parham Rd. ME4—2A 8
Park Av. ME7—2E 8
Park Av. ME14—1K 23
Park Av. ME17—6G 27
Park Cres. ME4—4A 8
Parker Clo. ME8—7B 10
Parkfield Rd. ME8—2C 10
Parkfields. ME2—4B 2
Park Ho. ME14—1K 23
Park La. ME14—7F 21
Park Mnr. ME7—6D 4
Park Rd. ME19—3B 18
Park View Ct. ME15—6C 24
Park Way. ME15—6K 23
Park Way. ME17—5E 26
Park Wood Ind. Est. ME15—4E 28
Park Wood Pde. ME15—5D 28
Parr Av. ME7—5E 4
Parsonage Cotts. ME15—2B 26
Parsonage Ct. ME19—6A 18
Parsonage La. ME2—2H 3
Partridge Av. ME20—3D 18
Pasley Rd. ME7—5B 4
Pasley Rd. E. ME4—4C 4
Pasley Rd. N. ME4—4C 4
Pasley Rd. W. ME4—4B 4
Patrixbourne Av. ME8—2K 9
Pattens Gdns. ME1—2J 7
Pattens La. ME4—2J 7
Pattens Pl. ME4—2J 7
Payne's La. ME15—1J 27
Pearman Clo. ME8—3D 10
Pear Tree Av. ME20—5G 19
Peartree La. ME3—3A 2
Pear Tree La. ME7—4F 9
Pear Tree La. ME15—2K 27
Pear Tree Row. ME17—3G 29
Pear Tree Wlk. ME9—7K 11
Peckham Clo. ME3—3H 3
Peel St. ME1—1J 23
Peggoty Clo. ME3—2A 2
Pelican Clo. ME2—5B 2
Pemberton Sq. ME2—3H 3
Pembroke Gdns. ME8—1G 17
Pembroke Rd. ME4—3B 4
Pembroke Rd. ME17—5D 26
Pembury Gdns. ME16—4F 23
Pembury Way. ME8—2B 10
Penenden Ct. ME14—7H 21
Penenden Heath Rd. ME14—7J 21
Penenden St. ME14—1J 23
Penfold Clo. ME5—5C 8
Penfold Clo. ME15—3C 28
Penfold Way. ME15—2H 27
Penguin Clo. ME2—5C 2
Pennant Rd. ME1—5H 7
Pennine Way. ME15—6E 28
Penshurst Clo. ME8—2B 10
Penstocks, The. ME15—5F 23
Pentagon Shopping Centre. ME4
—7A 4
Pepy's Way. ME2—3E 2
Perie Row. ME7—5B 4
  (off Middle St.)
Perimeter Rd. ME20—2G 19
Perryfield St. ME14—1H 23
Perry St. ME4—1K 7
Perry St. ME14—1H 23
Pested Bars Rd. ME17—3A 28
Peterborough Gdns. ME2—5B 2
Peterborough Ho. ME15—1B 28
  (off Cambridge Cres.)

Petham Grn. ME8—1K 9
Peverel Dri. ME14—2E 24
Pheasant La. ME15—1K 27
Pheasant Rd. ME4—2D 8
Phillips Ct. ME8—2J 9
Phoenix Rd. ME5—3H 15
Pickering St. ME15—2J 27
Pickwick Cres. ME1—2H 7
Pier App. Rd. ME7—4E 4
Pier Pl. ME2—1B 4
Pier Rd. ME7—4E 4
Pikefields. ME8—2K 9
Pilgrim Cotts. ME2—1C 12
Pilgrims Rd. ME2—4A 6
Pilgrims View. ME6—5D 12
Pilgrims Way. ME1—1J 13
Pilgrims Way. ME2—1B 6
  (Cuxton)
Pilgrims Way. ME2—4A & 2A 12
  (Upper Halling)
Pilgrims Way. ME14
—1E 20 to 3K 21
Pilot Rd. ME1—4H 7
Pimperney Way. ME5—1E 14
Pine Clo. ME20—4E 18
Pine Gro. ME7—7H 9
Pine Gro. ME14—1K 23
Pine Ho. ME5—7A 8
Pine Lodge. ME16—4E 22
Pine Rd. ME2—5E 2
Pinewood Dri. ME5—5K 15
Piper's Cotts. ME15—4G 27
Pippin Clo. ME17—6D 26
Pippincroft. ME7—6H 9
Pirbright Clo. ME5—3K 15
Pitt Rd. ME16—6D 22
Pitt Rd. ME17—5K 29
Place La. ME9—7G 11
Plains Av. ME16—5E 22
Plaistow Sq. ME14—1A 24
Plantation La. ME14—3E 24
Plantation Rd. ME7—5H 5
Platters, The. ME8—5K 9
Playstool Clo. ME9—6K 11
Playstool Rd. ME9—6K 11
Pleasant Row. ME1—6H 3
Pleasant Row. ME8—5B 4
Plomley Clo. ME8—1F 17
Plough Cotts. ME17—6H 29
Ploughmans Way. ME8—6B 10
Ploughwents Rd. ME17—6E 28
Plover Clo. ME5—4K 15
Plover Rd. ME20—4D 18
Pluckley Clo. ME8—1K 9
Plumpton Wlk. ME15—2D 28
Plumtree Gro. ME7—1C 16
Plum Tree Rd. ME9—5K 17
Plumtrees. ME16—5C 22
Poachers Clo. ME5—7D 8
Podkin Wood. ME5—5F 15
Poles, The. ME9—1H 11
Polhill Dri. ME5—3F 15
Police Sta. Rd. ME19—6A 18
Polmar Rd. ME16—1F 23
Pope St. ME16—5E 22
Poplar Av. ME2—6E 2
Poplar Gro. ME16—2E 22
Poplar Rd. ME2—6D 2
Popicans Rd. ME2—1A 6
Porchester Clo. ME15—2J 27
Port Clo. ME5—2H 15
Port Clo. ME14—2C 24
Porters Wlk. ME17—4J 29
Portland Pl. ME6—5E 12
Portland Rd. ME1—1G 13
Portland Rd. ME7—5F 5
Portland St. ME2—2C 8
Portsdown Clo. ME16—5D 22
Portsmouth Clo. ME2—5C 2
Post Barn Rd. ME4—2A 8
Postley Rd. ME15—6J 23
Potyn Ho. ME1—7H 3
Pout Rd. ME6—6D 12
Povey Av. ME2—1H 3
Powell Clo. ME20—3A 20
Powlett Rd. ME2—2H 3
Pratling St. ME20—3B 20
Precinct, The. ME1—6H 3
Premier Pde. ME20—5J 19
Preston Av. ME7—3F 9
Preston Way. ME8—2K 9
Pretoria Ho. ME15—3C 28
  (off Lubbock Clo.)
Pretoria Rd. ME4—2A 8
Pretoria Rd. ME7—1E 8
Pridmore Rd. ME6—5D 12
Priestfield Rd. ME7—6F 5
Priestfields. ME1—1G 7
Priestley Dri. ME20—2D 18
Primrose Av. ME8—7J 9
Primrose Clo. ME4—5K 7
Primrose Cotts. ME15—7F 25

Primrose Dri. ME20—5H 19
Prince Arthur Rd. ME7—5C 4
Prince Charles Av. ME5—1H 15
Princes Av. ME5—2F 15 to 5D 8
Princess Mary Av. ME4—4C 4
Prince's St. ME1—7H 3
Princes St. ME14—2J 23
Prinys Dri. ME8—1E 16
Priors Ga. ME1—6H 3
Priory Clo. ME16—7D 22
Priory Ct. ME8—2H 9
Priory Gro. ME20—5H 19
Priory Rd. ME2—5F 3
Priory Rd. ME8—2H 9
Priory Rd. ME15—4J 23
Prospect Av. ME2—3G 3
Prospect Pl. ME1—2F 7
Prospect Pl. ME16—6J 23
Prospect Row. ME4—1B 8
Prospect Row. ME7—5B 4
Provender Way. ME14—2C 24
Pudding La. ME14—3H 23
Pudding Rd. ME8—4C 10
Pump Clo. ME19—5B 18
Pump La. ME8—3K 9
Purbeck Rd. ME4—2K 7

Quarry Cotts. ME17—4K 27
Quarry Rd. ME15—5J 23
Quarry Rd. ME17—4K 27
Quarry Sq. ME14—2J 23
Quarry Wood Ind. Est. ME20,
—7J 19
Queen Anne Rd. ME14—3J 23
Queen Ct. ME1—7H 3
Queendown Av. ME8—7A 10
Queen Elizabeth Sq. ME15—2B 28
Queen Mother Ct., The. ME1—7G 3
Queens Av. ME6—5E 12
Queen's Av. ME16—2F 23
Queens Rd. ME5—2E 8
Queens Rd. ME6—5E 12
Queens Rd. ME7—7D 4
Queen's Rd. ME16—4D 22
Queen St. ME1—7H 3
  (in two parts)
Queen St. ME4—7B 4
Queenswood Rd. ME20—6D 14
Quickthorn Cres. ME5—7K 7
Quinion Clo. ME5—5G 15
Quinnell St. ME8—4C 10
Quixote Cres. ME2—2G 3

Raggatt Pl. ME15—5K 23
Ragstone Rd. ME15—5E 24
Railway St. ME4—7A 4
Railway St. ME7—6E 4
Rainham Clo. ME15—6J 23
Rainham Rd. ME5—1D 8
Rainham Shopping Centre. ME8
—3C 10
Raleigh Clo. ME5—6B 8
Ramillies Clo. ME5—6B 8
Randall Rd. ME4—3K 7
Randall St. ME14—1H 23
Randolph Cotts. ME2—2G 3
Randolph Rd. ME7—6D 4
Ranscombe Clo. ME2—6C 2
Raven Clo. ME20—5E 18
Ravenswood Av. ME2—3G 3
Rawdon Rd. ME15—4J 23
Raymer Rd. ME14—6H 21
Reach Row. ME7—4B 4
  (off Admiralty Ter.)
Reading Rd. ME15—3D 28
Readscroft Rd. ME8—7A 10
Recreation Av. ME6—5E 12
Recreation Clo. ME14—1K 23
Rectory Clo. ME6—5E 12
Rectory La. ME16—6C 22
Rectory La. N. ME19—4C 18
Rectory La. S. ME19—4C 18
Reculver Wlk. ME15—1D 28
Redbank. ME19—4C 18
Redbridge Clo. ME5—7D 8
Redcliffe La. ME14—7H 21
Rede Ct. Rd. ME2—3C 2
Rede Wood Rd. ME16—4A 22
Redfern Av. ME7—4F 5
Redsells Clo. ME15—6E 24
Redvers Rd. ME4—2B 8
Redwing Clo. ME20—3D 18
Redwood Clo. ME5—3H 15
Reform Rd. ME4—1C 8
Regency Clo. ME8—2E 16
Regent Dri. ME15—7J 23
Regent Rd. ME7—7C 4
Reginald Av. ME2—1B 6
Reginald Rd. ME16—4G 23
Reinden Gro. ME15—6D 24
Renown Rd. ME5—3J 15
Repton Way. ME5—1F 15

37

Reservoir Cotts. ME2—1C 12
Resolution Clo. ME5—6B 8
Restharrow Rd. ME14—3C 24
Retreat, The. ME15—4A 26
Revenge Rd. ME5—4J 15
Rhode St. ME4—7B 4
Rhodewood Clo. ME15—6E 24
Richard St. ME1—1H 7
Richard St. ME4—7A 4
Richmond Clo. ME5—1H 15
Richmond Rd. ME7—5D 4
Richmond Way. ME15—7J 23
Ridgeway, The. ME4—5K 7
Ridgeway, The. ME7—4D 4
Ridgway. ME16—5D 22
Ridley Rd. ME1—7G 3
Ringlestone Cres. ME14—6F 21
Ringwood Clo. ME4—4A 10
Ringwood Rd. ME15—7A 24
Ripon Clo. ME8—1A 10
Rise, The. ME1—1J 7
Rise, The. ME7—2C 16
River Clo. ME15—1C 26
River Dri. ME2—4D 2
Riverhead Clo. ME16—1F 23
Riverside E. Rd. ME4—2D 4
Riverside View. ME20—4B 20
River St. ME7—5B 4
River Way. ME20—2E 18
Roach St. ME2—4F 3
Roberts Orchard Rd. ME16—4B 22
Roberts Rd. ME6—5D 12
Roberts Rd. ME8—4B 10
Robin Hood La. Lower. ME5
            —4E 14 to 3G 15
Robin Hood La. Upper. ME5
            —4D 14
Robson Dri. ME20—4H 19
Rocfort Rd. ME6—5E 12
Rochester Rd. ME1—7H 3
Rochester Ho. ME15—1B 28
Rochester Rd. ME1—3J 13
Rochester Rd. ME1—7B 6
  (Wouldham)
Rochester Rd. ME2—3A 6
  (Cuxton)
Rochester Rd. ME7—7H 7
Rochester Rd. ME20
            —3A 20 to 7D 14
  (Aylesford)
Rochester St. ME4—2K 7
Rock Av. ME7—7D 4
Rock Rd. ME14—7G 21
Rocks Rd., The. ME19—7E 18
Rocky Hill. ME16—3G 23
Rocky Hill Ter. ME16—3G 23
Roebuck Rd. ME1—6H 3
Roffen Rd. ME1—2H 7
Rolvenden Av. ME8—1K 9
Rolvenden Rd. ME1—1H 3
Roman Heights. ME14—1A 24
Roman Rd. ME6—5D 12
Roman Way. ME2—7E 2
Romany Rd. ME8—2J 9
Romney Pl. ME15—4E 24
Romney Pl. ME15—3J 23
Romney Rd. ME6—6C 8
Romsey Clo. ME2—3D 2
Roosevelt Av. ME5—5A 8
Ropemakers Ct. ME4—3B 8
Roper Clo. ME8—2E 16
Rope Wlk. ME4—6A 4
Roseacre Gdns. ME14—3E 24
Roseacre La. ME14—2E 24
Roseberry Rd. ME4—2K 7
Rosebery Rd. ME4—4E 4
Rose Cotts. ME15—4H 27
  (off Old Salts La.)
Roseholme. ME16—5F 23
Roseleigh Av. ME16—3E 22
Rosemary Clo. ME5—1F 15
Rosemary Ct. ME2—4E 2
Rosemary Rd. ME15—4E 24
Rosemary Rd. ME19—5D 18
Rosemount Clo. ME15—4H 27
Rose St. ME1—1J 7
Rose Yd. ME14—1J 23
Ross St. ME1—7J 3
Rother Ho. ME15—7B 24
Rother Vale. ME15—2J 15
Roundhay. ME19—5B 18
Roundwell. ME14—3H 25
Rover Rd. ME5—3H 15
Rowan Clo. ME20—5J 19
Rowbrocke Clo. ME8—2F 17
Rowland Av. ME7—2F 9
Rowland Clo. ME7—3F 9
Royal Sovereign Av. ME4—4C 4
Royal Star Arc. ME14—3H 23
Royston Rd. ME15—4E 24
Roystons Clo. ME8—2C 10
Ruckinge Way. ME8—1K 9

Rudge Clo. ME5—3K 15
Rugby Clo. ME5—1F 15
Rush Clo. ME5—2G 15
Rushden Rd. ME2—6C 2
Rushmead Dri. ME15—1J 27
Ruskin Clo. ME19—6D 18
Russell Ct. ME4—1C 8
Russell Rd. ME20—6D 14
Russells Av. ME8—4D 10
Russett Clo. ME2—3D 2
Russett Clo. ME17—5E 26
Rutland Cotts. ME17—3J 29
Rutland Pl. ME2—2E 16
Rutland Way. ME15—7B 24
Ryan Dri. ME15—5E 24
Ryarsh La. ME19—5A 18
Ryarsh Rd. ME19—1A 18
Rycaut Clo. ME4—2F 17
Rydal Ho. ME15—1B 28
Ryde Clo. ME5—4C 8
Ryegrass Clo. ME5—6D 8

Sadlers Clo. ME5—3D 14
Saffron Way. ME5—7A 8
Sailmakers Ct. ME4—2C 8
St Albans Clo. ME4—4F 5
St Alban's Rd. ME2—5C 2
St Andrew's Clo. ME16—5C 22
St Andrew's Rd. ME7—4E 4
St Andrew's Rd. ME16—4C 22
St Anne's Ct. ME16—3G 23
St Asaph Ho. ME15—1B 28
  (off Middlesex Av.)
St Barnabas Clo. ME7—1E 8
St Bartholomews La. ME1—7K 3
St Bartholomews Ter. ME1—7K 3
St Benedict Rd. ME4—6C 12
St Clements Ho. ME1—6J 3
St David's Ho. ME15—1B 28
  (off Nottingham Av.)
St Edmunds Way. ME8—3E 10
St Faith's La. ME14—3F 25
St Faith's St. ME14—3H 23
St George's Rd. ME7—5D 4
St George's Sq. ME16—4F 23
St Helen's Cotts. ME15—7A 22
St Helen's La. ME15—7A 22
St Helier's Clo. ME16—5E 22
St James Clo. ME19—6D 18
St John's Clo. ME3—1B 2
St John's Rd. ME7—1D 8
St Johns Way. ME1—2G & 2F 7
  (in two parts)
St Katherine's La. ME6—6D 12
St Laurence Av. ME20—6B 20
St Leonards Av. ME4—2A 8
St Leonard's St. ME19—7A 18
St Lukes Av. ME14—2K 23
St Lukes Rd. ME14—2K 23
St Margarets Banks. ME1—6J 3
St Margaret's Clo. ME16—5D 22
St Margarets Dri. ME8—7K 9
St Margaret's Mews. ME1—6H 3
St Margaret's St. ME1—7G 3
St Mary's Ct. ME19—6A 18
St Mary's Gdns. ME4—4C 4
St Mary's Rd. ME14—4G 3
St Mary's Rd. ME7—5D 4
St Mary's Wlk. ME1—4K 13
St Matthews Dri. ME1—2F 7
St Michaels Clo. ME4—1A 8
St Michael's Clo. ME20—3C 20
St Michael's Rd. ME16—4F 23
St Paul's Clo. ME2—5C 2
St Peter's Clo. ME20—5F 19
St Peter's Rd. ME20—5F 19
St Peter St. ME1—7J 3
St Peter St. ME15—2H 23
St Philip's Av. ME15—4K 23
St Stephen's Cotts. ME15—2A 26
St Stephen's Sq. ME15—5G 23
St Williams Way. ME1—1J 7
Salem St. ME15—4J 23
Salisbury Av. ME8—4A 10
Salisbury Ho. ME15—1B 28
Salisbury Rd. ME4—1B 8
Salisbury Rd. ME14—1J 23
Salisbury Rd. ME20—5D 14
Sally Port. ME7—5B 4
Sally Port Gdns. ME7—5B 4
Saltings Rd. ME6—6E 12
Salts Av. ME15—5H 27
Salts Farm Cotts. ME15—4J 27
Saltwood Rd. ME15—6H 23
Samphire Clo. ME14—3C 24
Sanctuary Rd. ME8—1H 9
Sandbourne Rd. ME15—5F 21
Sandgate Ct. ME8—1H 17
Sandhurst Clo. ME8—1K 9
Sandling Ct. ME14—7H 21
Sandling La. ME14—5E 20
Sandling Rd. ME14—2H 23

Sandown Dri. ME8—5A 10
Sandown Rd. ME19—6A 18
Sandpiper Rd. ME5—3K 15
Sandringham Rd. ME8—1G 17
Sandycroft Rd. ME2—2E 2
Sandy Dell. ME7—2C 16
Sandy La. ME6—7C 12
Sandy La. ME14—2F 25
  (Bearsted)
Sandy La. ME14—6J 21
  (Penenden Heath, in two parts)
Saracen Clo. ME7—3H 9
Sassoon Clo. ME20—2E 18
Saunders St. ME4—1A 8
Saunders St. ME7—5D 4
Savage Rd. ME5—2H 15
Sawyers Ct. ME4—2B & 2C 8
Saxon Clo. ME2—2E 2
  (Broom Hill)
Saxon Clo. ME2—6E 2
  (Strood)
Saxons La. ME14—1K 23
Saxon Shore Way. ME3—1D 4
Saxon Shore Way. ME7—4H 5
Saxon St. ME7—6D 4
Scalett Clo. ME5—7D 8
School Av. ME7—7F 5
School La. ME1—7B 6
School La. ME3—3J 3
School La. ME9—1K 11
School La. ME15—6C 24
Scimatar Clo. ME7—3H 9
Scotby Av. ME5—1H 15
Scotney Ho. ME2—2H 3
  (off Cypress Rd.)
Scott Av. ME8—4D 10
Scott Clo. ME20—6G 19
Scotteswood Av. ME4—2A 8
Scott's Ter. ME4—1A 8
Scott St. ME14—1H 23
Scraces Cotts. ME16—7C 22
Scragged Oak Rd. ME14—7D 16
Scrubbs La. ME16—3F 23
Seagull Rd. ME2—5B 2
Seamew Ct. ME2—4B 2
Seaton Rd. ME7—1F 9
Seaview Rd. ME7—7D 4
Second Av. ME4—3C 8
Second Av. ME7—1F 9
Secretan Rd. ME1—3G 7
Sedge Cres. ME5—1E 14
Sedley Clo. ME8—2E 16
Sedley Clo. ME20—4K 19
Selbourne Rd. ME7—4E 4
Selby Rd. ME15—4D 28
Sellinge Grn. ME8—1K 9
Selstead Rd. ME8—2K 9
Senacre La. ME15—2C 24
Senacre Cotts. ME15—2D 28
Senacre Sq. ME15—1D 28
Sessions Ho. Sq. ME14—2H 23
Setford Clo. ME5—6D 8
Settington Av. ME5—3D 8
Severn Rd. ME5—7D 8
Sevington Pk. ME15—2H 27
Seymour Rd. ME5—1C 8
Seymour Rd. ME8—4F 11
Seymour's Cotts. ME17—1J 29
Shackleton Clo. ME5—6C 8
Shades, The. ME2—4A 2
Shaftesbury Clo. ME19—5D 18
Shaftesbury Dri. ME16—3E 22
Shakespeare Rd. ME7—7D 4
Shamley Row. ME5—3K 15
Shanklin Clo. ME5—4D 8
Sharnal La. ME6—6E 12
Sharon Cres. ME15—1F 15
Sharstead Way. ME7—2C 16
Sharsted Way. ME14—2F 25
Shatfleet Dri. ME14—4A 2
Shawstead Rd. ME5—5D 8 to 2K 15
Shaws Way. ME1—1H 7
Shaws Wood. ME2—2G 3
Sheal's Cres. ME15—5J 23
Shearers Clo. ME14—3C 24
Shelden Dri. ME8—4C 10
  (in two parts)
Sheldon Way. ME20—3E 18
Shelley Rd. ME16—5E 22
Shepherds Ga. ME7—7G 9
Shepherds Way. ME17—4J 29
Shepperton Clo. ME5—1J 15
Sheppey Rd. ME15—1J 27
Sheraton Ct. ME15—4F 15
Sherbourne Dri. ME16—5D 22
Sheridan Clo. ME5—5D 8
Sheridan Clo. ME14—6E 20
Sheridan Ct. ME1—2F 7
Sheriff Dri. ME5—3G 15
Sherman Clo. ME7—3J 9
Shernolds. ME15—1K 27
Sherwood Av. ME5—3G 15

Ship La. ME1—7K 3
Shipley St. ME14—3J 23
Shipwright Av. ME4—3B 8
Shirley Ct. ME15—3C 28
Shirley Way. ME15—4E 24
Sholden Rd. ME2—2H 3
Shoreham Wlk. ME15—1D 28
Shortlands Grn. ME15—3D 28
Short La. ME7—5H 5
Short St. ME4—1C 8
Shorts Way. ME1—2F 7
Shottenden Rd. ME7—4E 4
Shropshire Ter. ME15—1C 28
Shrubsole Rd. ME14—3F 21
Sidney Rd. ME1—2F 7
Sidney Rd. ME4—4D 4
Sidney St. ME16—5E 22
Silverdale. ME16—5B 22
Silverdale Dri. ME8—5C 10
Silver Hill. ME1—2E 6
Silver Hill. ME1—1A 8
Silverspot Clo. ME8—5C 10
Silverweed Rd. ME5—1E 14 & 7A 8
Simmons La. ME15—2F 29
Simpson Rd. ME8—7E 12
Sindal Shaw Ho. ME5—1E 14
Sindals La. ME5—5A 16
Singapore Dri. ME7—6B & 6C 4
Sir Evelyn Rd. ME1—3G 7
Sir Thomas Longley Rd. ME2
            —4K 3
Siskin Wlk. ME20—4D 18
Sittingbourne Rd. ME14—2K 23
Skeleton Hill. ME1—1H 13
Skene Clo. ME8—3D 10
Skinner St. ME4—1A 8
Skinner St. ME7—6D & 5D 4
Skinners Way. ME17—4J 29
Skura Ct. ME2—4B 2
Slade Clo. ME5—3H 15
Slatin Rd. ME2—3G 3
Slicketts Hill. ME4—7B 4
Smarden Wlk. ME8—3E 10
Smarts Ct. ME14—3G 25
Smith Rd. ME2—5F 3
Smith Rd. ME5—2H 15
Snipe Ct. ME2—4B 2
Snodhurst Av. ME5—7K 7
Snodhurst Ho. ME5—5A 8
Snodland By-Pass. ME6
            —7E to 4E 12
Snodland Rd. ME6—7A 12
Snowdon Av. ME14—2K 23
Snowdon Clo. ME5—5C 8
Snowdon Pde. ME14—2A 24
Solomon Rd. ME8—3C 10
Solomon's Rd. ME4—7A 4
Somerfield Clo. ME16—3F 23
Somerfield La. ME16—2F 23
Somerfield Rd. ME16—3F 23
Somerset Clo. ME5—4D 8
Somerset Rd. ME15—7A 24
Somner Wlk. ME15—4D 28
Sorrell Rd. ME8—1F 15
South Av. ME8—2H 9
Southbourne Gro. ME5—1G 15
S. Bush La. ME8—7E 10
South Cres. ME17—5E 26
South Eastern Rd. ME2—4H 3
Southey Way. ME20—2D 18
Southfields. ME1—1G 7
South Ga. ME1—5H 3
  (off Precinct, The.)
Southill Rd. ME4—1A 8
South Pk. Rd. ME15—6K 23
South Rd. ME7—4B 4
S. Side Two Rd. ME4—2C 4
South St. ME16—6A 22
South St. Rd. ME9—6J 17
South View. ME14—3G 25
Southwark Rd. ME7—3B 4
Southwell Rd. ME2—5B 2
Southwood. ME16—5B 22
Spade La. ME9—7F 11
Spearhead Rd. ME14—7F 21
Speedwell Av. ME5—1E 14
Speedwell Clo. ME14—3C 24
Spekes Rd. ME7—6J 9
Speldhurst Ct. ME16—3F 23
Spencer Clo. ME5—7B 8
Spencer Way. ME15—1C 28
Spenlow Dri. ME5—5G 15
Spillway, The. ME5—5F 23
Spindle Glade. ME14—2A 24
Spindlewood Clo. ME5—2H 15
Spinney, The. ME5—4G 15
Spinney, The. ME15—5K 23
Spires, The. ME2—6C 2
Spires, The. ME16—3F 23
Spitfire Clo. ME5—4K 23
Sportsfield. ME14—2K 23
Spot Farm Cotts. ME17—1H 29

Spot La. ME15—5D 24
Sprig, The. ME14—3E 24
Springett Clo. ME20—7K 13
Springett Way. ME17—4F 27
Springfield Av. ME14—7F 21
Springfield Rd. ME7—5F 5
Springfield Rd. ME20—2C 18
Springfield Ter. ME4—7A 4
Springvale. ME8—6K 9
Springwood Clo. ME16—4B 22
Springwood Rd. ME16—4C 22
Spruce Clo. ME20—4E 18
Spurgeon's Cotts. ME17—6G 27
Spurway. ME14—3E 24
Square Hill. ME15—3K 23
Square Hill Rd. ME15—4K 23
Squires Clo. ME2—4A 2
Stable Clo. ME5—7D 8
Staceys St. ME14—2H 23
Staffa Rd. ME15—1J 27
Stafford St. ME7—6C 4
Stag Rd. ME5—7D 8
Stake La. ME2—1B 12
Stalin Av. ME5—4C 8
Stampers, The. ME15—5F 23
Standen Clo. ME8—1G 17
Standgate Rd. ME6 & ME19—5A 12
Stanford Dri. ME16—4E 22
Stanford Way. ME2—2B 6
Stangate Rd. ME2—4B 2
Stanhope Clo. ME14—7E 20
Stanhope Rd. ME2—3F 3
Stanley Clo. ME5—6D 8
Stanley Rd. ME7—5D 4
Stanstead Clo. ME16—7C 20
Staplehurst Rd. ME8—1J 9
Star La. ME7—5H 9
Star Mill La. ME5—2E 8
Station App. ME16—4H 23
Station Hill Cotts. ME15—1D 26
Station Rd. ME2—2B 6
(Cuxton)
Station Rd. ME2—4G 3
(Strood)
Station Rd. ME8—4C 10
Station Rd. ME14—2H 23
Station Rd. ME15—7C 22
Station Rd. ME20—5G 19
Steele St. ME2—3F 3
Steerforth Clo. ME1—2H 7
Sterling Av. ME16—2E 22
Stevens Clo. ME6—5E 12
Stevens Clo. ME20—7K 13
Stevenson Way. ME20—2D 18
Stickens La. ME19—7C 18
Stirling Clo. ME1—1H 7
Stirling Rd. ME8—1G 17
Stockbury Dri. ME16—7D 20
Stockett La. ME17 & ME15
—5E 26 to 6G 23
Stockton Clo. ME14—6H 21
Stoneacre Clo. ME8—7A 10
Stoneacre Cotts. ME15—1G 29
Stoneacre La. ME15—7F 25
Stone Cotts. ME15—1B 26
(East Farleigh)
Stone Cotts. ME15—6B 24
(Maidstone)
Stone Cotts. ME17—4F 29
Stonecross Rd. ME5—3D 8
Stonehorse La. ME3—1F 3
Stoney Hill. ME5—1C 8
Stony La. ME5 & ME1—7G 7
Stopford Rd. ME7—7D 4
Stour Clo. ME2—4D 2
Stour Ho. ME15—7B 24
Strand App. Rd. ME7—4F 5
Stratford Av. ME8—4A 10
Stratford La. ME8—4C 10
Straw Mill Hill. ME15—6G 23
Streamside. ME20—5G 19
Stream, The. ME20—5G 19
Street End Rd. ME5—4C 8
Streetfield Rd. ME8—3C 10
Street Rd. ME2—2H 3
Street, The. ME2—1C 12
Street, The. ME7—4D 16
Street, The. ME9—7G 11
(Hartlip)
Street, The. ME9—1K 11
(Lower Halstow)
Street, The. ME9—1H 11
(Upchurch)
Street, The. ME14—3G 25
Strover St. ME7—4D 4
Stuart Clo. ME14—1K 23
Stuart Rd. ME7—1E 8
Sturdee Av. ME7—7F 5
Sturla Rd. ME4—2B 8
Sturry Way. ME8—2K 9
Style Clo. ME8—1G 17
Stylewood Clo. ME1—4G 7

Suffolk Av. ME8—3C 10
Suffolk Rd. ME15—7B 24
Sugarloaf Hill. ME5—2E 8
Sultan Rd. ME5—4J 15
Sunderland Clo. ME1—1F 7
Sunderland Sq. ME8—4D 10
Sundridge Dri. ME5—1G 15
Sundridge Hill. ME2—1B 6
Sunningdale Clo. ME8—6A 10
Sunningdale Ct. ME15—3K 23
Sunningdale Dri. ME8—6A 10
Sunnyfields Clo. ME8—4B 10
Sunnymead Av. ME7—6F 5
Sunnyside. ME8—3G 25
(off Street, The.)
Sun Ter. ME5—1H 15
Surrey Rd. ME15—7B 24
Sussex Clo. ME5—1G 15
Sussex Heights. ME5—4F 15
Sussex Rd. ME5—6B 24
Sutherland Gdns. ME8—6B 10
Sutton Rd. ME15—7K 23
Sutton Rd. ME17—1B 28 to 6H 29
Sutton St. ME14—4H 25
Swain Rd. ME8—6J 9
Swale Ho. ME15—1C 28
Swale Rd. ME2—4B 2
Swallow Rise. ME5—7B 8
Swallow Rd. ME20—4D 18
Swan Clo. ME2—3E 2
Swan St. ME19—6A 18
Swift Clo. ME20—4E 18
Swift Cres. ME5—6C 8
Swingate Clo. ME5—3H 15
Sycamore Cres. ME16—2E 22
Sycamore Dri. ME20—5J 19
Sycamore Rd. ME2—6D 2
Sydney Rd. ME4—1B 8
Sylvan Glade. ME5—5G 15
Sylvan Rd. ME8—4K 9
Symons Av. ME4—2A 8

Tadburn Grn. ME5—1H 15
Taddington Wood La. ME5—3E 14
Tail Race, The. ME15—5G 23
Talbot Dri. ME2—5E 2
Talbot Rd. ME16—1E 22
Tamar Dri. ME2—5E 2
Tamar Ho. ME15—7C 24
Tamarind Clo. ME7—1C 16
Tangmere Clo. ME7—6G 5
Tanker Hill. ME8—6A 10
Taswell Rd. ME8—3D 10
Tatler Clo. ME5—3K 15
Taverners Rd. ME8—5A 10
Tavistock Clo. ME5—4F 15
Tavistock Clo. ME8—5B 10
Tay Clo. ME5—7C 8
Taylor Rd. ME6—6D 12
Taylor's La. ME2—4G 3
Taylors La. ME8—1B 2
Teapot La. ME20—4J 19
Teasaucer Hill. ME15—7H 23
Teasel Rd. ME5—1F 15
Tedder Av. ME5—5B 8
Tees Ho. ME15—1C 28
Telegraph Hill. ME8—3B 2
Telford Ho. ME14—2J 23
Temeraire Mnr. ME7—5B 4
(off Middle St.)
Temple Gdns. ME2—5E 2
Temple St. ME2—4F 3
Temple Way. ME19—6D 18
Tennyson Rd. ME7—1D 8
Tenterden Clo. ME5—7C 8
Terminus Rd. ME16—5C 22
Tern Cres. ME2—5B 2
Terrace Rd. ME16—3G 23
Terrace, The. ME1—6H 3
Terrance Clo. ME4—2B 8
Terry's Yd. ME14—3J 23
Test Ho. ME15—7C 24
Teynham Grn. ME8—7H 5
Thackeray Rd. ME20—3D 18
Thames Av. ME8—4B 10
Thames Ho. ME15—7B 24
Thanet Ho. ME15—3D 28
Thanet Rd. ME8—1E 16
Theodore Pl. ME7—6D 4
Third Av. ME8—3D 8
Third Av. ME7—1F 9
Thirlmere Clo. ME2—2H 3
Thirlmere Ho. ME7—6H 5
Thistlebank. ME5—2G 15
Thistledown Clo. ME7—1C 16
Thomas St. ME1—1H 7
Thomson Clo. ME6—4E 12
Thorndale Clo. ME5—7J 7
Thorndike Ho. ME4—4A 8
Thornham Rd. ME8—1K 9
Thornhill Pl. ME14—1J 23
Thorold Rd. ME5—1C 8
Thorpe Wlk. ME8—2E 16

Thrale Way. ME8—1G 17
Threshers Dri. ME14—2B 24
Thurnham La. ME14—2F 25
Tichborne Clo. ME16—1E 22
Tichfield Clo. ME15—2D 28
Tichfield Rd. ME15—2D 28
Tideway, The. ME1—3H 7
Tilbury Rd. ME8—2D 10
Timber Tops. ME5—4K 15
Tintagel Mnr. ME7—5D 4
Tintern Rd. ME16—7C 20
Tobruk Way. ME5—6A 8
Toddington Cres. ME5—4D 14
Toledo Pl. ME7—6E 4
Tomlin Rd. ME6—5E 12
Tonbridge Ct. ME16—4F 23
Tonbridge Ho. ME2—2H 3
(off Cypress Rd.)
Tonbridge Rd. ME16
—6A 22 to 4G 23
Toronto Rd. ME7—7F 5
Tovil Grn. ME15—6G 23
Tovil Hill. ME15—6G 23
Tovil Rd. ME15—5H 23
Tower La. ME14—3E 24
Town Hall. ME19—5A 18
Town Hill Clo. ME19—5A 18
Townsend Rd. ME6—5C 12
Trading Est. 20/20. ME20—6B 20
Trafalgar St. ME7—6D 7
Transom Ho. ME1—3H 7
Trapfield Clo. ME14—3G 25
Trapfield La. ME14—3G 25
Trapham Rd. ME16—2F 23
Travertine Rd. ME5—4H 15
Trelawn Cres. ME5—3H 15
Trellyn Clo. ME8—5B 22
Trent Ho. ME15—1C 28
Trenton Clo. ME16—7B 20
Trent Rd. ME5—7C 8
Trevale Rd. ME1—3G 7
Trevino Dri. ME5—2F 15
Trevor Dri. ME16—1D 22
Trewin Clo. ME20—4H 19
Trident Clo. ME2—4K 3
Trinity Ct. ME20—3A 20
Trinity Rd. ME7—5D 4
Troodos Hill. ME14—6F 21
Trotwood Clo. ME5—5G 15
Truro Clo. ME8—1A 10
Truro Ho. ME15—1B 28
Tudor Av. ME14—1K 23
Tudor Cotts. ME15—4G 27
Tudor Gro. ME8—4B 10
Tufa Clo. ME5—4H 15
Tufton Rd. ME8—3C 10
Tufton St. ME14—3J 23
Tunbury Av. ME5—3F 15
Tunbury Av. S. ME5—4F 15
Turgis Clo. ME17—4J 29
Turkey Ct. ME15—3A 24
Turnstone Rd. ME5—3J 15
Tuscan Dri. ME5—4J 15
Twisden Rd. ME16—4F 23
Two Post All. ME1—5H 3
Twydale Grn. ME8—1J 9
Twydall La. ME8—2J 9
Twyford Clo. ME8—2D 10
Twyford Ct. ME14—1B 24
Tydeman Rd. ME15—5D 24
Tyland Cotts. ME14—3E 20
Tyland La. ME14—3E 20
Tyler Clo. ME19—6D 18
Tyler Dri. ME8—1G 17
Tyne Clo. ME5—7D 8
Tyne Ho. ME15—2C 28

Ufton Clo. ME15—6C 24
Ulcombe Rd. ME17—5J 29
Ullswater Ho. ME15—1B 28
Undercliff. ME15—4H 23
Underdown Av. ME4—3A 8
Underwood Clo. ME15—5H 23
Unicumes La. ME16—5E 22
Union Pl. ME4—7B 4
Union St. ME1—6H 3
Union St. ME14—3J 23
Unwin Clo. ME20—3A 20
Upbury Rd. ME4—7K 3
Uplands Clo. ME2—5C 2
Upnor Rd. ME2—3J 3 to 1A 4
Up. Barn Hill. ME5—5A 26
Up. Britton Pl. ME7—6C 4
Up. Carisbrooke Cotts. ME15
—6H 23
Up. East Rd. ME4—4C 4
Up. Fant Rd. ME16—5E 22
Up. Hunton Hill. ME15—5C 26
Up. Luton Rd. ME5—1D 8
Upper Rd. ME15—5K 23
Up. Stone St. ME15—4J 23

Upper St. ME17—4K to 1K 29
Urquhart Clo. ME5—7B 8

Vale Dri. ME5—7J 7
Valence Ho. ME15—1A 28
Valentine Clo. ME7—3H 9
Valentine Rd. ME15—1C 28
Valerian Clo. ME5—1E 14
Vale Rd. ME15—4G 27
Valiant Rd. ME5—3J 15
Valley Dri. ME15—3H 27
Valley Rise. ME5—3F 15
Valley Rd. ME7—7F 5
Valley, The. ME17—5F 27
Valley View Rd. ME1—3G 7
Vange Cottage Mews. ME1—7G 3
Vanity La. ME17—7F 27
Varnes St. ME20—7K 13
Vauxhall Cres. ME6—7D 12
Veles Rd. ME6—5D 12
Ventnor Clo. ME5—4D 8
Vicarage Clo. ME2—2B 12
Vicarage Clo. ME20—3K 19
Vicarage La. ME15—1D 26
Vicarage Rd. ME2—2A 12
(Halling)
Vicarage Rd. ME2—3G 3
(Strood)
Vicarage Rd. ME7—6D 4
Vicary Way. ME16—2F 23
Victoria Clo. ME5—3D 14
Victoria Pde. ME14—2H 23
Victoria Rd. ME4—2C 8
Victoria Rd. ME5—3D & 3E 14
(in two parts)
Victoria St. ME1—6J 3
Victoria St. ME2—4G 3
Victoria St. ME7—6D 4
Victoria St. ME16—4G 23
Victoria St. ME20—7K 13
Victoria Ter. ME1—2F 7
Victory Mnr. ME7—5B 4
(off Middle St.)
Viking Clo. ME2—7E 2
Villa La. ME3—2A 2
Vincent Rd. ME20—6C 14
Vine Cotts. ME17—5E 26
Vineries. ME7—6G 5
Vines La. ME1—6H 3
Vinters Rd. ME14—3K 23
Vintners Way. ME14—3C 24
Violet Clo. ME5—5G 15
Virginia Rd. ME7—4D 4
Vixen Clo. ME5—6D 8
Vulcan Clo. ME5—5C 8

Waghorn Rd. ME6—5E 12
Waghorn St. ME4—1C 8
Wagoners Clo. ME14—3C 24
Wainscott Eastern By-Pass ME2
—1J 3
Wainscott Rd. ME2—1J 3
Wainscott Wlk. ME2—1J 3
Wakefield Clo. ME2—5B 2
Wakeley Rd. ME8—3D 10
Wake Rd. ME1—4H 7
Walderslade Centre. ME5—2G 15
Walderslade Rd. ME4 & ME5—4A 8
Walderslade Rd. ME5
—6A 8 to 3F 15
Walderslade Woods. ME5
—2D 14 to 5J 15
Waldron Dri. ME15—3H 27
Wallace Rd. ME1—4K 7
Wallbridge La. ME8—1F 11
Wallers Cotts. ME15—4B 26
Wallis Av. ME15—3C 28
Walmer Ct. ME14—2J 23
Walmer Ho. ME2—2H 3
(off Cypress Rd.)
Walmers Av. ME3—1A 2
Walnut Clo. ME5—4C 8
Walnut Tree Av. ME15—3J 27
Walnut Tree Cotts. ME15—3J 27
Walnut Tree Ct. ME20—5F 19
Walnut Tree La. ME15—3J 27
Walpole Clo. ME19—5D 18
Walsham Rd. ME5—4F 15
Walshaw Ho. ME14—1J 23
Walsingham Clo. ME8—2F 17
Walsingham Ho. ME14—1J 23
Walter Burke Av. ME1—7B 6
Waltham Rd. ME8—1J 9
Warbler's Clo. ME2—4F 3
Warden Clo. ME16—3E 22
Warden Ct. ME16—3F 23
Warden Rd. ME1—2H 7
Warde's Cotts. ME15—7F 25
Ware St. ME14—2E 24
Warlingham Clo. ME8—3D 10
Warmlake Rd. ME17—7F 29
Warner St. ME4—1A 8

Warnford Gdns. ME15—7J 23
Warren La. ME9—2K 17
Warren Rd. ME20—5D 14
Warren Wood Rd. ME1—5H 7
Warwick Cres. ME1—2E 6
Warwick Pl. ME16—4G 23
Washington Ho. ME15—3C 28
Water La. ME14—3H 25
Water La. ME15—3J 23
Water La. ME19—6A 18
Waterloo Rd. ME7—7D 4
Waterloo St. ME15—4J 23
Waterlow Rd. ME14—1J 23
Watermeadow Clo. ME7—6G 9
Water Mill Clo. ME2—3H 3
Waterside. ME14—2H 23
Waterside La. ME7—4G 5
Waters Pl. ME7—6H 9
Water Works Cotts. ME1—4F 7
Waterworks Cotts. ME14—1D 24
Watling Av. ME5—2E 8
Watling St. ME2—3A to 4E 2
Watling St. ME5 & ME7—2E 8
Watson Av. ME5—7J 7
Watts Almshouses. ME1—7H 3
Watts Av. ME1—7H 3
Watts St. ME4—1K 7
Waveney Ho. ME15—7C 24
(off Westmorland Clo.)
Waverley Clo. ME5—3K 15
Waverley Clo. ME17—6E 26
Way Clo. ME5—7D 8
Wayfield Rd. ME5—5A 8
Wayne Ct. ME2—1J 3
Weald Clo. ME5—3A 28
Weavering Cotts. ME15—4C 24
Weavering St. ME14—3C 24
Webster Rd. ME8—3C 10
Weeds Wood Rd. ME5—1F 15
Week St. ME14—2J 23
Welcombe Ct. ME8—4A 10
(off Derwent Way.)
Welland Rd. ME15—7C 24
Weller Av. ME1—2J 7
Wellington Ho. ME15—3D 28
Wellington Pl. ME14—1H 23
Wellington Rd. ME7—7D 4
Well Rd. ME2—2J 23
Wells Ct. ME2—6C 2
Wells Ho. ME15—1B 28
Wells Rd. ME2—6C 2
Well St. ME15—4G 27
Well St. ME19—7C 18
Wemmick Clo. ME1—5J 7
Wents, The. ME15—5C 26
Wentworth Dri. ME8—5B 10
Wesley Clo. ME16—4B 22
Westbrook Clo. ME4—2B 8
Westcourt St. ME7—5B 4
West Dri. ME5—7J 7
Westergate Rd. ME2—2E 2
Westerham Clo. ME8—7J 5
Westerhill Rd. ME17—7E 26
Western Rd. ME16—5D 22
Westfield Cotts. ME9—2K 11
Westfield Sole Rd. ME14—5J 15
West Malling By-Pass. ME19
—7A 18

Westmarsh Clo. ME15—1D 28
W. Mill Rd. ME20—3G 19
Westmorland Clo. ME15—1C 28
Westmorland Grn. ME15—1C 28
Westmorland Rd. ME15—1C 28
Westmount Av. ME4—7A 4
Weston Rd. ME2—4F 3
West Pk. Rd. ME15—5K 23
Westree Rd. ME16—4G 23
West Rd. ME4—2B 4
West Rd. ME7—4B 4
West St. ME2—2G 3
West St. ME7—5E 4
West St. ME15—7B 26
West St. ME19—6A 18
W. View Cotts. ME17—6G 29
West Wlk. ME16—4D 22
Westway. ME17—5E 26
W. Wood La. ME9—6J 17
Westwood Rd. ME15—1J 27
Wetheral Dri. ME5—1H 15
Weybridge Clo. ME5—1J 15
Weyhill Clo. ME14—1B 24
Wharf Rd. ME7—4D 4
Wharf Rd. ME15—5G 23
Whatman Clo. ME14—1A 24
Wheatcroft Gro. ME8—5C 10
Wheatfield. ME19—5C 18
Wheatfields Way. ME14—3B 24
Wheatsheaf Clo. ME15—7K 23
Wheeler St. ME14—2J 23
Wheeler St. Hedges. ME14—7H 21
Whiffen's Av. ME4—6A 4
Whiffen's Av. W. ME4—6A 4
Whimbrell Clo. ME20—4D 18
Whimbrell Wlk. ME5—4J 15
Whitchurch Clo. ME16—3G 23
Whitcombe Clo. ME5—3J 15
Whitebeam Dri. ME17—5D 26
Whitedyke Rd. ME6—3B 12
White Ga. ME2—2E 2
Whitegate Ct. ME8—7A 10
Whitehall Rd. ME14—1K 25
Whiteheads La. ME14—3F 25
White Hill Rd. ME9—4F 17
Whitehorse Hill. ME5—1C 8
White Horse La. ME15—2E 28
Whitehouse Cres. ME1—5A 14
White Leaves Rise. ME2—1A 6
White Rd. ME4—3B 8
White Rock Pl. ME16—4G 23
Whitewall Rd. ME2—3J 3
Whitmore St. ME16—5E 22
Whittaker St. ME4—7B 4
Whyman Av. ME4—3B 8
Wicken Ho. ME16—3G 23
Wickham Clo. ME9—6K 11
Wickham St. ME1—1J 7
Widgeon Rd. ME2—5C 2
Wierton Rd. ME17—6C 28
Wigmore Rd. ME8—7J 9
Wilberforce Rd. ME17—5F 27
Wildman Clo. ME8—2F 17
Wildwood Glade. ME7—1D 16
Will Adams Way. ME7—3G 9
William Rd. ME2—2B 6
William St. ME8—3D 10
Willington Grn. ME15—1C 28

Willington St. ME15—1C 28
Willis Cotts. ME7—5C 16
Willowby Gdns. ME8—1G 17
Willow Cottage. ME2—1B 12
Willow Ct. ME15—2J 27
Willow Ho. ME5—1F 15
Willow Mead. ME19—4C 18
Willow Rd. ME2—5D 2
Willow Rd. ME20—3D 18
Willows, The. ME8—2B 10
Willows, The. ME9—6K 11
Willow Way. ME15—4K 23
Wilmecote Ct. ME8—4A 10
(off Derwent Way.)
Wilmington Way. ME8—2J 9
Wilson Av. ME1—3J 7
Wilson Clo. ME15—1C 28
Wilsons La. ME15—4C 26
Wilton Dri. ME20—6F 19
Wiltshire Clo. ME5—4D 8
Wiltshire Way. ME15—7C 24
Wimbourne Dri. ME8—6A 10
Winchelsea Rd. ME5—7C 8
Winchester Av. ME5—1F 15
Winchester Ho. ME15—1B 28
Winchester Pl. ME14—2J 23
(off Bluett St.)
Winchester Way. ME8—3D 10
Windermere Dri. ME8—5A 10
Windermere Ho. ME15—1B 28
Windmill Clo. ME2—2G 3
Windmill La. ME19—7A 18
Windmill Rd. ME7—1C 8
Windmill St. ME2—2G 3
Windsor Clo. ME14—1K 23
Windsor Rd. ME4—2A 8
Windsor Rd. ME7—6E 4
Windward Rd. ME1—3H 7
Windyridge. ME7—3F 9
Wingham Clo. ME8—1K 9
Wingham Clo. ME15—1D 28
Wingrove Dri. ME14—2C 24
Winifred Rd. ME15—4D 24
Winston Dri. ME2—1J 3
Winston Rd. ME2—1J 3
Winterfield La. ME19—6C 18
Wirrals, The. ME5—1G 15
Witham Way. ME2—4E 2
Wittersham Clo. ME5—7C 8
Wivenhoe Clo. ME8—2D 10
Wolfe Rd. ME16—5D 22
Wollaston Clo. ME8—2F 17
Wolletts Cotts. ME17—5E 26
Woodbury Rd. ME5—4E 14
(in two parts)
Woodchurch Cres. ME8—2K 9
Woodcut. ME14—6G 21
Woodcutt Cotts. ME17—5K 25
Woodford Rd. ME16—5D 22
Woodhouse Clo. ME20—2D 18
Woodhurst. ME5—1D 14
Woodhurst Clo. ME2—2A 6
Woodland Clo. ME14—7H 21
Woodlands. ME5—3G 15
Woodlands. ME17—5D 26
Woodlands Av. ME6—5D 12
Woodlands Rd. ME7—2G 9
Woodlands Rd. ME20—5G & 6H 19

Woodland Way. ME14—7H 21
Woodlea. ME19—4D 18
Woodleas. ME16—5B 22
Woodpecker Glade. ME8—6A 10
Woodpecker Rd. ME20—5D 18
Woodside. ME8—6J 9
Woodside Rd. ME15—1A 28
Woodstock Rd. ME2—4F 3
Wood St. ME2—2A 6
Wood St. ME7—4B 4
Woodview Rise. ME2—2E 2
Woodville Rd. ME15—5J 23
Woolaston Clo. ME15—6H 23
Wooldeys Rd. ME8—2C 10
Woolett St. ME14—2J 23
Woolley Rd. ME15—7C 24 to 2D 28
Woolwich Clo. ME5—5B 8
Wootton Grn. ME8—1A 10
Wopsle Clo. ME1—5J 7
Worcester Clo. ME2—3D 2
Worcester Rd. ME15—1B 28
Wordsworth Clo. ME5—5D 8
Wordsworth Rd. ME14—7H 21
Wordsworth Way. ME20—2E 18
Workhouse La. ME15—3E 26
Wotton Clo. ME15—3C 28
Wouldham Rd. ME1—4C 6
Wrangleden Clo. ME15—3C 28
Wrangleden Rd. ME15—3C 28
Wren Clo. ME20—4D 18
Wren Ind. Est. ME15—4D 28
Wren Way. ME5—6C 8
Wyatt Pl. ME2—4F 3
Wyatt St. ME14—3J 23
Wykeham Cotts. ME17—6H 27
Wykeham Rd. ME2—3G 3
Wyke Manor Rd. ME14—3J 23
Wyles Rd. ME4—2K 7
Wyles St. ME7—4D 4
Wyndham Rd. ME4—2K 7
Wyvern Clo. ME20—6E 12
Wyville Clo. ME8—7B 10

Yalding Clo. ME2—2G 3
Yantlet Dri. ME4—4B 2
Yarrow Rd. ME5—1E 14
Yaugher La. ME9—3K 17 to 7F 11
Yelsted La. ME9—4H 17
Yelsted La. ME14—6J 15
Yelsted Rd. ME9—6K 17
Yeoman Ct. ME14—4F 25
Yeoman Dri. ME7—3G 9
Yeoman La. ME14—4F 25
Yeoman Way. ME15—5E 24
Yew Tree Clo. ME5—4K 15
Yew Tree Clo. ME20—5J 19
Yewtree Ind. Est. ME20—4H 19
Yew Tree Pl. ME7—4D 16
Yew Trees Ho. ME14—4J 21
York Av. ME5—2E 14
York Av. ME7—7C 4
York Hill. ME5—2D 8
York Ho. ME15—1B 28
(off Leicester Rd.)
York Rd. ME1—1H 7
York Rd. ME15—5K 23

Zetland Av. ME7—2F 9

Printed by THE **KPC** GROUP London and Ashford, Kent